CITIZENSHIP
A Christian Calling

CITIZENSHIP
A Christian Calling

BY LON FENDALL

BARCLAY PRESS
NEWBERG, OREGON

CITIZENSHIP: A Christian Calling

© 2003 by Lon Fendall

Published by
BARCLAY PRESS
Newberg, Oregon 97132
www.barclaypress.com

Cover design by Dan Jamison
ISBN 1-59498-000-4
Printed in the United States of America

CONTENTS

FOREWORD

Lon Fendall knows that Christianity is a call to citizenship in a way that few others do. Christ calls us to love one another. When we look around at the frenzy of human activity in today's earthly kingdom, we must ask where this stewardship of communication and caring has gone. What values guide us in our endless and complacent pursuit of power, prosperity, and place? Have we lost our way? Lon Fendall takes us to Scripture, then to modern lessons some people have learned in their lives of public service.

This collection of stories brings us home again from our present feelings of exile in our own land. Values lived by real people translate and speak to many as we yearn for a sense of community and faith-based interaction with each other in troubled times. These stories are for those who are frustrated by the prevalent push in today's world for individual and collective wealth when our souls are starving for the spiritual meaning of our mission on earth. These messages will challenge and disturb, yet bring hope and promise to those willing to remain faithful and to believe in the unseen when others all around us seek tangible, material evidence and reward.

Scripture calls us to be citizens, and we still can be! We can study and learn from our Christian roots, from biblical literature and from its people. There are problems today; there have always been problems. But this unique volume of faith and action calls us to unite in citizenship. I am honored to be included among its pages and humbled by my colleague's comparison of my endeavors to those of British Parliamentarian William Wilberforce. In public service, we Christians strive to balance our two worlds —

the spiritual internal life and the political external place of our vocational calling. It is a constant challenge and one that Lon Fendall has lived himself. He recognizes the value of sharing what we have learned with one another.

Young men and women often ask me how to pursue a life in public service and active Christian citizenship. There is no simple answer. But I recommend the biblical and modern stories in this instructive collection as one starts down that path. There is power and promise in this volume. There are tools for leadership and for teams of dedicated followers. There is ageless wisdom and revitalization in remembering the miracle of creation and our Maker's plan for us.

Mark O. Hatfield
U.S. Senator, retired
September 2003

I agreed to teach a Sunday school class, "Biblical Principles Regarding Government and Politics." The class members and I examined the political issues in different periods of Hebrew history. We began with the patriarchs, then continued with the Exodus leaders, the judges, the kings, and the prophets. We talked about how often political events occurred "in the gates" where leaders went to find each other and talk about the issues of the day. There, leaders found a place to exchange gossip, to plot against kings. Godly people could speak out for justice and righteousness. The Sunday school class members helped me clarify ideas I had been thinking about for several years.

While these ideas were incubating, three airliners changed course and headed toward three large and important buildings. We Americans learned from this terrible experience that we could no longer remain aloof from the political chaos in the world. In late 2001 there existed a greater need than ever to call Christians to the best of their faith, to find antidotes to extremism, to find clearer explanations of what it means to be a follower of Christ and a public citizen.

A number of other factors began to influence the shape of this book. I was impressed with the way Bruce Wilkinson introduced us to an obscure biblical character named Jabez in his book *The Prayer of Jabez*.[1] I knew from preparing for my Sunday school class that other little-known people in the Bible could teach us important principles of active Christian citizenship—people such as Jehoshaphat, Hezekiah, Mordecai, and Absalom. The lives of other well-known individuals—Solomon, Joseph, Nehemiah, and

Gideon—could also teach us about citizenship. Some of those people were kings, some were appointed officials, and some were private citizens who showed the impact godly people could have on governments. A number of the biblical figures were heroes, but others were miserable failures.

I began asking the biblical characters what they had to say to modern Christians about being active citizens. They had plenty to say, and I enjoyed giving voice to these biblical characters in the chapters that follow. I've had a sense of standing in the hall of statuary in the U.S. Capitol with the marble figures joining in a conversation. I stood in a circle of great and wise people, "surrounded by a cloud of witnesses" (Hebrews12:2).

I noted an important thing about the circle: I found my place on the perimeter, not in the center, joining with others discussing what it means to be a Christian citizen. Parker Palmer in his important book *The Courage to Teach*, describes the ideal teaching/learning situation as a "community of truth," which can be represented as a circle. Around the perimeter of the circle stand those seeking to know, some of them with more experience than others, but all sharing a desire to relate to, to interact with the subject of their inquiry. In the book, Palmer says,

> As we try to understand the subject in the community of truth, we enter into complex patterns of communication—sharing observations and interpretations, correcting and complementing each other, torn by conflict in this moment and joined by consensus in the next. The community of truth, far from being linear and static and hierarchical, is circular, interactive, and dynamic.[2]

While interacting with the biblical personalities in this circle, I determined that I should invite others to join the circle. The first choice was a person I had come to know and admire as I worked on another book project. This person, William Wilberforce, loved God, was energized and sustained by his faith in Christ, and accomplished astounding things in his career in politics.[3] I was delighted to discover that Wilberforce had many important things to say about the issues the biblical characters had introduced in our discussion.[4] Those thoughts are expressed in the selections in many of the chapters that follow.

As I studied the life of William Wilberforce, I found something strikingly familiar about his life and his ideas. I had the sensation I had met him before. Then it hit me. In amazing ways my former employer, Senator Mark Hatfield, had relived the life of William Wilberforce. The two men served in different countries and in very different eras, but they are very much alike. Both found a personal relationship with Christ after they were well established in a political career. Both found a close circle of Christians who helped them grow spiritually and supported them in prayer. Both experienced intense resistance in causes that seemed hopeless at times. Both were passionate about the application of biblical principles to the justice issues of their day. Both spoke boldly about their faith in Christ. Both remained active in political life for many years in spite of the unpopular positions they took. It was as if I looked around the circle of biblical figures, then turned to Wilberforce, and all nodded in agreement that Mark Hatfield should be invited to join the conversation. Like Wilberforce, Hatfield had spoken in several of his books to the issues in the life stories of the biblical characters in the circle.

I thank Liz Heaney for the idea of inviting a number of contemporaries to join our conversation. She said we needed to hear from people who have been active citizens in a variety of ways, but not in such prominent positions as Wilberforce and Hatfield. She suggested I include people with whom the readers could identify, people who went beyond thinking about biblical citizenship to acting on those ideas. It has been rewarding to invite these people to join our circle. They are garbage collectors, judges, philosophers, school board members, jurors, and prosecutors. Young and old, male and female, they are members of different denominations. They have earned their place in the circle by the fascinating ways in which they have served Christ as active citizens.

I'll never forget the day my family and I finished loading our U-Haul truck, ready to leave for Washington, D.C., to work for Senator Hatfield. We stood together in front of our house in Newberg, Oregon, saying our goodbyes to my parents, Kenneth and Rose Fendall. My father had passed his seventieth birthday and was having some health problems. He was sad to see his youngest son and youngest grandchildren traveling across the country to work full time in politics. But his greatest desire for all seven of his children was that we commit our lives to God and follow God's leading completely. Raelene and I felt sure God was leading us into this new type of citizenship, so my father was willing to send us on our way with tears and prayers. My dad died not long after that, but his zeal for the Lord's work has profoundly influenced my life. So it's an honor to dedicate this book in part to my father, Kenneth Fendall. During the final stages of preparing this book for printing, my mother, Rose Fendall, went to be with Jesus after living for 102 years. Her coaching in leadership skills, her prayers, and her encouragement have been very influential in my life. Thanks, Mom and Dad, for all you did to shape the qualities that have been part of my life as a citizen.

CHAPTER ONE

The Call to
Active Christian Citizenship

What an amazing inaugural day in Jerusalem! The people shouted at the top of their lungs, "Long live King Solomon!" Things seemed disorganized; there had not been much time to plan the festivities. David had abruptly decided it was time for his son, Solomon, to succeed him as king of Israel. The anointing process was short and simple. Solomon arrived in a strikingly informal manner, riding one of the royal mules. Zadok the priest brought out the ceremonial oil and poured it on Solomon's head. People grabbed whatever musical instruments they could find and organized a parade. The sound of their instruments, their shouting, and their singing was so exuberant it literally shook the streets of Jerusalem. Unfortunately, David was too ill to join in the festivities, but from his bed he could hear the celebrating and he praised God for such a promising beginning to his son's rule (1 Kings 1:28-48).

Fast-forward a short time and note the events at Gibeon, the town a few miles from Jerusalem where the Hebrew tabernacle was located during the building of the temple. Spiritually, Solomon had made a shaky start as leader of the Hebrew nation. He had refused to get rid of some of the counterfeit religious practices, especially the worship of pagan gods in the high places. But in this case, Solomon got his spiritual act together. To remove any doubt about his commitment to Jehovah God, he offered a thousand burnt offerings at the tabernacle's altar at Gibeon. He was determined to spare no expense to express the depth of his love for God.

Clearly, God accepted the sincerity of Solomon's worship, for God came to visit Solomon in Gibeon in an amazing dream. In the dream God extended to Solomon the greatest offer any ruler could have wanted and Solomon made the greatest response any king might have made. The offer, a blank check from the God of the universe, gave Solomon the opportunity to request absolutely anything he wanted. Think of what Solomon might have requested, especially since he was not in the best place spiritually. He could have asked for the ability to conquer and rule the entire Middle Eastern world. He could have asked that the public treasures never be exhausted. He could have asked to be surrounded by adoring subjects and beautiful, submissive women. Actually, he acquired most of those things later, not entirely in ways that honored God. But at Gibeon, Solomon remembered his father's dying words to him:

> "So be strong, show yourself a man, and observe what the Lord your God requires: Walk in his ways, and keep his decrees and commands, his laws and requirements, as written in the Law of Moses, so that you may prosper in all you do and wherever you go, and that the Lord may keep his promise to me: 'If your descendants watch how they live, and they walk faithfully before me with all their heart and soul, you will never fail to have a man on the throne of Israel.'" (1 Kings 2:2-4)

What a wonderful charge David had given Solomon and what a wonderful preparation for a momentous decision Solomon was about to make. Jehovah God has just offered him the choice of anything in the universe. He could be as selfish or as selfless as he chose. The angels in heaven paused in their songs of praise to see what this king would request from God's unlimited resources. Even as we read the passage, we hold our breath as we wait along with the angels for the answer. And at last we breathe easier when we hear the humble tone in Solomon's first words. Three times Solomon spoke of himself as God's servant. He even compared his lack of experience and political insight to that of a little child. *All right!* He must have been paying attention during the sacrifices earlier that day. He had focused on the majesty of God and realized how puny he was before God. He recognized that he was clueless about what it would take to be a good king.

And then came the decisive moment in this dialogue between Jehovah God and the newly inaugurated king of Israel. Having recognized his complete inadequacy to rule effectively without God's help, Solomon rejected the many frivolous choices he might have made and selected the things he needed most:

✓ A discerning heart.

✓ The ability to distinguish between right and wrong.

Way to go, Solomon! The earth shook as the Hebrew people celebrated his anointing. Then when Solomon selected God's wisdom and discernment as the things he most needed, the heavens shook with the singing of angels. The exuberance of the heavenly choir was far greater than anything Solomon's well-wishers had been able to manage (1 Kings 3:4-9).

Solomon framed his request very well and God gave him what he asked and a lot more. The essence of God's gift to Solomon was a "wise and discerning heart." Not wanting to place any limits on the gift, God gave Solomon "a breadth of understanding as measureless as the sand on the seashore." Then to reward Solomon for making such an appropriate choice, God threw in a package of extras including long life, wealth, and world acclaim (1 Kings 3:10-14; 4:29-34).

Fast-forward again to a later stage in Solomon's life. Among the indications of the wisdom and discernment God gave Solomon were thousands of wise statements and promises, now recorded in the book of Proverbs. The proverbs covered an immense range of topics. And as we would expect, the greatest political leader of his time had important things to say about how his subjects ought to seek the discernment and wisdom God gave to Solomon.

The first part of the book of Proverbs expresses the qualities of godly wisdom in the voice of a person, using the feminine gender. In chapter 1 we find this description of wisdom coming to the places public policy is discussed and decided:

> Wisdom calls aloud in the street, she raises her voice in the public squares; at the head of the noisy streets she cries out, in the gateways of the city she makes her speech. (Proverbs 1:20-21)

In this proclamation, Solomon drew on his knowledge of the public discourse of the day and localized the work of citizenship in the public squares, the busy streets, and the city gates. The typical city in Old Testament times had massive walls and gates to deter attacks. The gates were normally made of wood, often decorated with brass and iron. Since a constant flow of people came through these gates, the spaces near the gates became the logical place to take care of business, exchange news and gossip, and, to use a modern expression, find out "what's happening." Also religious events were held at the gates, sometimes to honor the pagan gods (2 Kings 23:8). In a more appropriate spiritual event held at one of the Jerusalem gates all the Hebrew people gathered to hear Ezra the scribe read the holy scriptures in celebration of the rebuilding of Jerusalem's walls (Nehemiah 8:1-3).

Along with all the other transactions that happened near the city gates, by Solomon's time these areas had become the places disputes were solved and political decisions made. The nation's elders were specifically charged with gathering at the gates to hear cases and make appropriate decisions (Deuteronomy 25:7-10). In the time of Esther, during the exile in Persia, the king's officials regularly gathered at the gates (Esther 3:2).

So Solomon spoke in the context of contemporary political culture when he called on godly people to declare God's wisdom in the streets, the public squares, and especially in the gateways of the city. Succeeding portions of the book of Proverbs provide the content of the messages to be delivered by godly people at the

Early in his career Senator Mark Hatfield called on Christians to participate in politics.

"I don't think that a person has to compromise his principles, his Christian faith, to become active in a political party—Democrat or Republican. I believe an attitude has probably sprung up within the Christian church, especially within the evangelical church, that there is something sinister or worldly about politics, especially to the extent that a person thus associated is not living the so-called separated life. I would like to make a point of theology here about the scriptural teaching on the separated life and on the Christian in the world. There is a vital and important difference between separation and isolation, and I think too many times evangelical Christians have confused isolation with separation.

"I think it's a poor Christian witness wherever we have less than excellence as a characteristic of the life of the witness. So, I would say a Christian in government or in teaching or in business or in anything else should represent the ultimate in excellence. This comes through education, through experience, and through participation. A Christian should enter in and be the best citizen. This doesn't mean every Christian has to go out and file for political office, but every Christian ought to be alert to the issues of the day, aware of the problems of his community. He ought to have the knowledge and the information necessary to establish a position, and then he ought to be active in helping to find solutions to these problems."[5]

gates. Among the more helpful of these messages are these familiar verses:

Trust in the Lord with all your heart and lean not on your own understanding; in all your ways acknowledge him, and he will make your paths straight. Do not be wise in your own eyes; fear the Lord and shun evil. (Proverbs 3:5-7)

What wonderful advice from a great king! What great advice for the citizens as well as the kings!

The prophet Jeremiah also spoke of the significance of the city gates as the places one can be an effective citizen. God directed Jeremiah to spend time at the gates, for there one could encounter the kings and the people as well. God gave Jeremiah a very simple and direct message: "Hear the word of the Lord, O kings of Judah and all people of Judah and everyone living in Jerusalem who come through these gates" (Jeremiah 17:20).

The words of Solomon and the call to Jeremiah shape the call to active, godly citizenship today. That call can be summarized as follows:

To be "in the gates" is to get involved in the discourse regarding public policy, to deal with the issues of the day and to bring God's love and truth to bear on those problems. Every believer is called of God to exercise some form of active citizenship.

Walls and gates still existed in the major cities in Jesus' day, but they were no longer the primary places political decisions were made. In Jesus' day the Romans exercised their control over Palestine from impressive public buildings and they were not about to allow the voices of the citizens to influence them. The Jewish leaders had places for the Sanhedrin to meet, functioning as a shadow government. And of course the Jewish leaders were not much more interested in listening to the people than the Roman officials. But the New Testament echoes the same "in the gates" teachings as the Old Testament, that all serious followers of God are to function as active citizens. We will explore details of that teaching in the succeeding chapters of this book, but Romans 12 and 13 build an important foundation for that teaching.

We can condense the call to active Christian citizenship found in Romans 12:

✓ First experience a spiritual and moral transformation.

✓ Exercise your gifts in appropriate ways, whether serving others, teaching, or in leadership roles, which may include public service.

✓ Live in loving devotion to others.

✓ Extend forgiveness to those who persecute you.

✓ Provide tangible help to those in need, even to those labeled as

**William Wilberforce calls on the followers of
Christ to be godly citizens.**

"Let true Christians, with becoming earnestness, strive in all
things to recommend their profession and to put to silence the
vain scorn of ignorant objections. Let them boldly assert the
cause of Christ in an age when so many who bear the name of
Christian are ashamed of Him. Let them accept the duty to
serve, if not actually to save their country. Let them serve not
by political interference, but by that sure and radical benefit of
restoring the influence of true religion and of raising the
standard of morality.

"Let them be active, useful, and generous toward others. Let
them show moderation and self-denial in themselves. Let them
be ashamed of idleness. When blessed with wealth, let them
withdraw from the competition of vanity and be modest,
retiring from ostentation, and not be the slaves of fashion. Let
them be moderate in all things. Let them cultivate a catholic
spirit of general good will and of kindness toward others. Let
them encourage men of real piety—wherever they may be
found—and others to repress vice and revive and spread the
influence of real Christianity. Let them pray earnestly for the
renewal of its vitality.

"May there be here at least a sanctuary, a land of true faith and
piety, where we may still enjoy the blessings of Christianity.
May there be here in this nation a place where the name of
Christ is still honored and men may see the blessings of faith in
Jesus. May the means of religious education and consolation
once again be extended to surrounding countries and to the
world at large."[6]

enemies.

✓ Function harmoniously in human society.

✓ Live the life of the peacemaker.

✓ Respond to evil behavior with good actions.

Based on this foundation of right living in Romans 12, Romans 13 goes on to speak in very positive terms about Christian citizenship. Part of this teaching applies to every Christian and part of it to those who in the previous chapter were identified as having gifts of leadership, specifically in government. In Romans 13 and in a similar passage in 1 Peter 2:13-17, we find a set of imperatives for Christian citizenship:

✓ By doing good, one is true to one's conscience and eliminates any need to be afraid of punishment from civil authorities.

✓ One's public conduct should reflect his or her commitment to being God's servant.

✓ One should respect, honor, and submit to those in positions of civil authority.

✓ One should treat other citizens with respect and love.

✓ One should pay taxes and other fees without hesitation.

The list of expectations for those who are chosen for civil leadership is shorter than the "must do" list for ordinary Christian citizens, at least in these passages. The rulers are instructed to:

✓ Punish those who do wrong.

✓ Honor those who do right.

✓ Function as God's servants (the same phrase used by King Solomon).

A number of other teachings in Scripture give guidance to godly rulers; these will be explored in coming chapters. But that simple phrase, "servants of God," contains a great deal of meaning. It indicates that God affirms the vocation of civil leadership and calls on public servants to function with a servant mind-set and ethos.

The New Testament call to Christian citizenship is captured in the phrase "God's servant," used repeatedly in Romans 13. Some Christians are called to serve God as "public servants," as politicians, government staff, and civil servants of various kinds.

All Christians are called to be "God's servants" in the myriad ways they can serve as active citizens.

What does it mean to be God's servants in public life? Many things, but at least these:

✓ To use one's influence to direct public resources toward those individuals and communities with the greatest needs.

✓ To conduct one's self publicly and privately in a way that honors God and encourages citizens to live uprightly.

✓ To be a godly influence, whether in cities, counties, states, or nations, toward treating neighboring jurisdictions with respect and goodwill.

The Bible says a great deal about the duties of Christian citizenship. There are duties to pray faithfully and appropriately, to respect the officials, to willingly pay taxes. The Bible additionally sets forth central priorities for citizen and official alike: compassion, justice, peacemaking, prophetic courage, integrity, and servanthood. We will explore these principles in this book.

MEET EZRA KOCH

We had speakers in chapel at least twice a week while I was in college. Most have faded from my memory. Of the few I can still recall, one chapel speaker stands out as an example of an active and effective Christian citizen. What an amazing man Ezra Koch was and is. I remember being startled when the person introducing Ezra in chapel at George Fox called him a "garbage collector." Actually, he had long since stopped collecting the garbage himself at the time he spoke in chapel. He owned City Sanitary and Recycling, based in McMinnville, Oregon.

His business was keeping small communities clean. His passion was serving Jesus in any way he could. He talked in chapel about the opportunity to impact one's government through praying for and witnessing to government leaders. He talked about the impact of his friend Doug Coe, who had gone out of his way to witness to Mark Hatfield and to guide him from casual church membership to passionate faith in Jesus. Ezra told us about the

Prayer Breakfast movement that Doug Coe had helped found and the way the movement ministered to the nation's and the world's leaders. Ezra told us we could make a difference in our world by caring about political leaders and by being active citizens ourselves.

A few years later when I decided to get more actively involved in politics, I met Ezra again, practicing what he had preached. When it was time for a Mark Hatfield reelection campaign, Ezra was always the Yamhill County chairman. Ezra and Mark were brothers in Christ and they trusted each other. But Ezra did more than just pray for his friend. He worked at mobilizing people in every community in the county to inform their neighbors about the senator's candidacy and to urge them to vote. He knew how to organize an event that guaranteed a good turnout to hear the senator. Hatfield always preferred a volunteer-based campaign to the high-cost, low-involvement campaigns built around TV ads and opinion polls. People like Ezra made the Hatfield campaigns work.

Ezra has now sold his garbage business and retired and Senator Hatfield has retired as well, but Ezra continues to do what he can to exercise the love of Christ in the political arena. And undoubtedly he influenced many others the way he did me, to become more active citizens and in so doing to spread the love of Christ in politics and government.

CHAPTER TWO

Praying for Government Leaders

"Michele, this has been a difficult week in our nation. Will you lead us in prayer for our president and other government leaders?"

"Of course, Pastor Gary. Lord Jesus, today we bring to you our president. Please help him carry the heavy burdens of our nation. Help him and his advisors to seek your face when they lack wisdom and courage. Help them to lead godly lives, and may they be an example to all our nation. Bless our nation. May it live up to its godly heritage.

"In Jesus' precious name, amen."

A good prayer? Definitely. God can bless any sincere prayer. Does God intend that believers pray for their government leaders? By all means. Does Michele's prayer measure up to the biblical teaching on praying for government leaders? Maybe, maybe not. But if the prayer left something to be desired, who could blame Michele, since there has not been much teaching on this subject? How many Christians realize that Scripture contains excellent model prayers showing how the godly leader ought to pray and how the active Christian citizen ought to pray for their leaders in government? Are these model prayers hidden away in the Bible? Not really. Like decorated eggs at an Easter egg hunt for toddlers, they are hidden in plain sight.

The Model Prayer for the Government Leader on Behalf of the People

Jehoshaphat was what could be called an "outlier," a rare exception to the generalization that the Hebrew kingdoms of Israel and Judah suffered from terrible political leaders.

God had warned them, of course, but the Hebrews were determined to follow the conventional wisdom of the day that it was not possible to hold a nation together and defend it without a king. God reluctantly went along with the request that a kingdom be set up, predicting that the people would soon put their trust in their government and their armies, not in God. After rebellion split the nation, the kings of Israel fulfilled God's prediction exactly. Their spiritual qualities and their leadership ability ranged from bad to terrible. Old Testament accounts of these kings are depressing to read.

Jehoshaphat and a handful of the kings of Judah, Israel's neighbor to the south, broke away from paganism to provide godly leadership. As recorded in 2 Chronicles 19 – 20, Jehoshaphat did some great things. He instructed his subordinates to make every decision with a keen awareness of their reliance on God: "Consider carefully what you do," he advised his leaders, "because you are not judging for man but for the Lord, who is with you whenever you give a verdict" (2 Chronicles 19:6). He set up a system we today would call "conflict management," designating trusted people to settle disputes.

When faced with an attack from an alliance of Moabites, Ammonites, and Meunites, Jehoshaphat turned away from swords and spears to the only weapon that would have been effective, prayer and fasting. His prayer (2 Chronicles 20:6-12) is a great model for the godly leader to renew and express his or her trust in God:

> "O Lord, God of our fathers, are you not the God who is in
> heaven? You rule over all the kingdoms of the nations. Power
> and might are in your hand, and no one can withstand you."

Senator Mark Hatfield on prayer for governmental leaders

"On the basis of the material we have briefly examined, I think we can summarize certain basic biblical principles which should guide the Christian in his or her relationship to any State. First, there is the clear scriptural admonition, mentioned often, to pray for those in authority. Such prayer, in my view, should recognize that the rulers of this world find themselves faced, usually unconsciously, with the temptations of power resulting from the spiritual warfare raging in the world. I know such talk sounds foreign and strange to our modern, secular culture; yet, I am convinced that such biblical insight has a deep relevance to this era. Those in positions of authority need our prayers not only for wisdom in facing difficult decisions, but also so that the State may resist those cunning and persistently powerful temptations which would make it an instrument of evil, rather than let it seek its intended and humble place in the divine order of things."[7]

Notice the focus on praise to God for who God is. The advancing armies possessed intimidating power but were puny in the sight of the great God of the universe.

"O our God, did you not drive out the inhabitants of this land before your people Israel and give it forever to the descendants of Abraham your friend?"

Jehoshaphat reaffirmed the covenant, first expressed to Abraham and treasured by those among the Hebrews who were fully obedient to God. The examples of God's deliverance in the past were many, especially during the Exodus. Jehoshaphat did not list those; God knew of these events and certainly those hearing the prayer did as well.

"They have lived in it and have built in it a sanctuary for your Name, saying, 'If calamity comes upon us, whether the sword of judgment, or plague or famine, we will stand in your presence before this temple that bears your Name and will cry out to you in our distress, and you will hear us and save us.'"

Jehoshaphat's trust in God's power to deliver the Hebrew people is amazing. He said in his prayer that their true hope lay in doing exactly what they were doing, gathering at the place of worship to call on God. Nothing more, nothing less.

> "But now here are men from Ammon, Moab and Mount Seir, whose territory you would not allow Israel to invade when they came from Egypt; so they turned away from them and did not destroy them. See how they are repaying us by coming to drive us out of the possession you gave us as an inheritance."

Jehoshaphat and his people had a problem and it was not a little problem. They were about to be slaughtered. But Jehoshaphat understood that it was God's problem not his own. God had directed that these non-Hebrews be spared. Now Jehoshaphat gently reminded God it was time to come to their rescue.

> "For we have no power to face this vast army that is attacking us. We do not know what to do, but our eyes are upon you."

Effective praying leads the one who prays to the place of complete helplessness. Jehoshaphat had reason to fear the complete extinction of the kingdom of Judah, its armies, and its top leaders. He named his fears and threw himself and his people into the hands of a God with unlimited strength. That was exactly the right thing to do.

And what about the rest of the story? After more praying and assurances of God's deliverance, the army of Judah set off for the battlefield. But instead of putting the strongest warriors at the head of the Judean army, Jehoshaphat selected the best singers in the kingdom to lead the army in songs of praise to God. As with the battles led by Joshua and Gideon, this was God's battle, not one to be fought by Judean soldiers. Not a single Judean sword or spear was to be raised against the enemies. God turned the enemies against each other and the soldiers completely destroyed each other. In one of the most dramatic statements in all of Scripture, the account in Chronicles tells us that a battlefield littered with all the enemy's dead bodies awaited the armies of Judah.

William Wilberforce urges people to pray

"Let them pray continually for their country at this time of national difficulty. We bear the marks only too plainly of a declining empire. Who can say how intercession before the Governor of the universe may avert for a while our ruin. It may appear before the eyes of the world foolishness for real Christians so to pray, yet we believe from Scripture that God will be disposed to favor the nation to which His servants belong.

"Boldly I must confess that I believe the national difficulties we face result from the decline of religion and morality among us. I must confess equally boldly that my own solid hopes for the well-being of my country depend, not so much on her navies and armies, nor on the wisdom of her rulers, nor on the spirit of her people, as on the persuasion that she still contains many who love and obey the Gospel of Christ. I believe that their prayers may yet prevail."[8]

The battle was the Lord's and he had won. *What an amazing God! What a wonderful prayer, releasing God to be victorious* (2 Chronicles 20:20-30).

A Model Prayer by the People on Behalf of the Government Leader

Jehoshaphat's prayer offers an excellent example of the effective prayer of a king or president on his or her own behalf. Scripture also provides us with a very good model prayer for the citizen and subject to pray on behalf of their leaders. Surprisingly, it is rarely noticed and seldom used as an outline for our prayers for political leaders. Not surprisingly, the prayer comes from one of the great political figures in the Bible (Psalm 72). The content of this prayer of King Solomon takes us far beyond the inadequacies of the "Lord, bless the president" prayers.

> Endow the king with your justice, O God, the royal son with your righteousness.

The prayer begins with a common theme in the Old Testament, the request that the king treat people as they deserve to be treated, as individuals created by God.

> He will judge your people in righteousness, your afflicted ones with justice. The mountains will bring prosperity to the people, the hills the fruit of righteousness. He will defend the afflicted among the people and save the children of the needy; he will crush the oppressor. He will endure as long as the sun, as long as the moon, through all generations. He will be like rain falling on a mown field, like showers watering the earth. In his days the righteous will flourish; prosperity will abound till the moon is no more.

Here we are given some real substance for our praying for government leaders. The ideals of justice and righteousness are fleshed out, indicating that these are not simply spiritual characteristics but they characterize the way those in power should treat those who are weak and helpless. The results of this right treatment are made clear—prosperity and longevity for ruler and subjects alike. The government leader becomes the source of great blessing, as beautiful as a gentle rain.

> He will rule from sea to sea and from the River to the ends of the earth. The desert tribes will bow before him and his enemies will lick the dust. The kings of Tarshish and of distant shores will bring tribute to him; the kings of Sheba and Seba will present him gifts. All kings will bow down to him and all nations will serve him.

We want a righteous and just leader to be honored and we want that person's leadership to be extended as far as possible. Therefore, the key prayer here is that the leaders will practice justice and righteousness.

> For he will deliver the needy who cry out, the afflicted who have no one to help. He will take pity on the weak and the needy and save the needy from death. He will rescue them from oppression and violence, for precious is their blood in his sight.

At this point the prayer returns to the concrete evidences of justice and righteousness. The prayer expresses an assumption that the powerful and wealthy will have the means to care adequately for themselves. The godly leader gives his or her attention to the needs of the weak, the victims, and the oppressed. The ungodly king cares only about his own power and wealth. Our prayer is that the leader will reverse these values and rescue those who would die without the help of the government.

> Long may he live! May gold from Sheba be given him. May people ever pray for him and bless him all day long. Let grain abound throughout the land; on the tops of the hills may it sway. Let its fruit flourish like Lebanon; let it thrive like the grass of the field. May his name endure forever; may it continue as long as the sun. All nations will be blessed through him, and they will call him blessed.

The prayer then turns to the great blessings we want for the one who fully meets God's expectations. There is no limit to the good things we want such a leader to experience.

> Praise be to the Lord God, the God of Israel, who alone does marvelous deeds. Praise be to his glorious name forever; may the whole earth be filled with his glory. Amen and Amen.

This is a powerful benediction to this prayer for government leaders. Its closing phrase takes us from our limited, nationalistic focus and leads us to call God's blessing on the entire world.

New Testament Teaching to Pray for Government Leaders

Teachings in the New Testament that call us to pray for our leaders echo the Old Testament prayers by and for government leaders. The most significant such New Testament passage is 1 Timothy 2:1-2. The apostle Paul began with calling on believers to pray for everyone, then seemed to stop midsentence to single out those in governmental leadership. This emphasizes the point that Christians have a special calling to pray for their leaders. It would have helped if Paul had expanded on his reasons for this type of prayer. He simply predicted that having godly leaders would make it possible for people to live peaceful and holy lives. He implies a passive role for government leaders—staying out of the way, doing as little as possible. But his brief comment does not provide a complete thought on the rationale for praying for those in government leadership. Our spirit should be drawn back to the teaching in Psalm 72 that the leader is the guardian of the poor and weak, exercising the government's power in active ways.

How to Pray for Government Leaders

✓ Base prayers on an attitude of respect toward government leaders, even if we disagree with their policies and positions.

✓ Pray for public officials by name, not just by position.

✓ Get acquainted with at least one public official so we can pray for specific requests he or she might give us.

✓ Pray that these public officials base their actions on justice and righteousness, as outlined in Psalm 72.

✓ Be obedient to any actions the Holy Spirit brings to our mind as we pray.

✓ When a public official is having difficulty, pray for him or her with greater determination rather than joining others in condemnation.

KARIN JORDAN

on the healing work of prayer at Ground Zero:

"What I'm sharing with you is about an ordinary person who believes in the power of prayer. I've been a Christian for over twenty years and I spend much time praying, trying to discern God's will for me, for the everyday things as well as the big things. There are many big things that have happened in my life, but I want to focus on just one this morning, one in which prayer had an essential role.

"I'm sure we all know exactly where we were the morning of September 11. I watched the attack on television and immediately felt the need to turn it over to the Lord. I prayed a lot during the next few hours and days, for the people on the planes that crashed and the people in the twin towers. I prayed for the people who jumped, the people who died or were injured, and the people who lost a loved one, the citizens of New York, and the whole country. I prayed that God would use me, as He had done previously in healing work after the Oklahoma City bombing and after the tragedy at Columbine High School. God's first answer to my prayer this time was an opportunity to work with Northwest Medical Teams, talking with people at Pioneer Square in downtown Portland, Oregon. Then, a few days later, I was invited to New York to help out. I trusted the Lord and He gave me peace and assurance that He had a plan in my going there.

"My part of the overall response plan was to help the students at a Christian college just a few blocks away from Ground Zero. We prayed with many of the students and listened to their stories. Some saw the first plane hit Tower One and then the second plane hit Tower Two. They saw people jump and die. They saw the injured, the burned, and the dead. They saw people running for their lives, away from the World Trade Center. They lost loved ones. They lost the sense of security that all Americans had before September 11.

"We talked, listened, and prayed. Some of the students were able to reach out and tell people about their faith and as they did that, prayer became an important part of the healing journey. But God didn't stop there! His plan for us was bigger. He opened the doors for us to go to Ground Zero at a time when it was tightly guarded by the military and police. It was only a week after the attack and the buildings were still burning. Everyone was wearing masks. We wore hard hats as we walked toward the ruins of an assault that had taken so many lives so very violently.

"As I walked and prayed, asking God to use me, I was struck by the number of firefighters and police officers there were. It seemed they were everywhere. What hit me was not so much the debris, but the fire trucks covered with posters of missing people from Tower 1 and 2. My heart ached for each and every one of them. I prayed some more. There was nothing I could do or say. I asked the Lord to use me. As we stopped at a street corner at Ground Zero, I remember being amazed again by how many firefighters and police officers were there, waiting for their next shift, sitting, standing, some trying to rest on stretchers. Some were in small groups, others alone. I started looking more closely into their faces and into their eyes. There was so much pain and sadness. There were so many of them, I couldn't imagine how I could help.

"Then I began to pray, 'God guide me.' Then I noticed a young firefighter, sitting alone, with his head down. I walked over to him, not sure what to do or say, asking for God's guidance. I sat next to him and started talking to him. He looked at me, and I will never forget the enormous sadness and hopelessness in his eyes. He told me he had been at Ground Zero for a week. He kept repeating that they had not found anyone alive. His eyes were filled with tears as he said, 'We have to keep on looking.' I said: 'You must be tired.' He nodded his head. 'You must have seen some pretty terrible things over the last week,' I said. He very slowly nodded his head. I prayed for guidance. Then I said: 'Can I pray for you?' Without any hesitation he said, 'Yes.' I prayed a short prayer and then was called to rejoin my group. Before I left I told this young firefighter that I would keep on praying for him. For just a few seconds our eyes met and he said very softly, 'Thanks.'

"After I left the firefighter, I asked God to protect each of these brave men and women in the days, weeks, and months ahead. And scarcely a day has since gone by that the memory of that young firefighter has not prompted me to pray for him and his fellow workers. Today, their work is almost finished at Ground Zero, but they have a long grieving and healing process ahead of them. They've seen so much and so many of them are having a difficult time dealing with what they have seen. We need to pray for them, and for our own local police and firefighters, thanking God for their selfless service to us all."[9]

CHAPTER THREE

Balancing Respect
with Accountability

Their eyes were adjusted to the darkness of the cave, so David's warriors could easily see without being seen. The lookout stationed near the front of the cave ran to tell David the great news.

"David, you're not going to believe who is using our cave as a rest room. It's none other than King Saul, your archenemy! Who can doubt that God has brought him right here to you, so you can at last put an end to his hatred and jealousy. Praise be to the God of Abraham for answering our prayers!"

"Don't be so quick to decide what God would have us do in this situation, my friend. I don't want anyone to unsheathe his sword. Don't move an inch from where you are. I'll go see for myself if it is Saul who has come to pay us a visit."

The men waited and waited, hardly daring to breathe, hearing nothing except the dripping of water from the ceiling of the cave. A time or two the fluttering wings of bats startled them. Then they saw David coming out of the shadows to rejoin them.

"So, did you turn his rest stop into a permanent rest, David? Can we send out the word that Saul is dead and you can assume your rightful place as God's anointed king of Israel?"

"You will do no such thing. Saul is very much alive. He's a heavy sleeper, so I had no problem getting close enough to cut this piece of cloth from his robe. But all the way back I felt bad that I was tempted to run my sword straight through him. You may think he fully deserves such a death, but God has rebuked me for these vengeful thoughts. I know Saul hates me and is jealous of my success. I know he feels threatened by the fact that Samuel has already anointed me to be the next king of Israel. But that spirit of hatred in Saul is not what God would have him feel toward me, nor me toward him.

"Saul has not been himself for years, since he has surrendered himself to the evil inside. He has been unable to realize I wish him no harm. Yes, our God is a God of justice and he will have his way with Saul at some point. But neither you nor I will lift our hand to bring the slightest harm to Saul. Our God is a God of love and forgiveness. When I take the throne, we must restore the worship of the true God, who would not have us take his justice into our own hands. This man is still our king. Yes, I have been anointed as well, but until God chooses to remove Saul as our king, I will serve and respect him and you will do the same." (See 1 Samuel 24.)

Time after time David had opportunities to punish King Saul for his abusive and undeserved treatment. This was the same David whose music had soothed Saul's raging emotions. This was the same David who was like a brother to Saul's son, Jonathan. David loved and respected his king so much that the news of Saul's death at a later time overwhelmed him with sorrow. "How the mighty have fallen," David sang. "Weep for Saul," he directed the people. His sorrow for the death of his king was no less than for his dear friend, the king's son, who died in the same battle. "Saul and Jonathan—in life they were loved and gracious, and in death they were not parted" (2 Samuel 1:17-27).

But we can learn another lesson from the episode in the cave. After cutting off a piece of Saul's robe and telling his men to put up their weapons, David did an unusual thing. He had completely obeyed the teachings Jesus later expressed about loving our enemies, but he also chose to confront Saul about his murderous crusade.

"Hey, King Saul!" David called out from the mouth of the cave after Saul had gone on his way. If Saul had not known that voice so well he might have assumed someone was playing a nasty trick on him. David was standing where Saul had just stood. Saul, assuming that David had armed men with him, would have had no explanation for the fact that David had not taken advantage of his helplessness.

David began with a gesture of deep respect, bowing before King Saul, making it clear this was not some trick with men hiding behind the rocks about to ambush Saul. David put into practice the biblical teaching about respecting those in governmental leadership. But David also exercised accountability toward Saul for Saul's undeserved and inappropriate efforts to kill him. To emphasize his point, David held up the piece of Saul's robe, showing how easy it would have been to kill the sleeping Saul. This was an "oops" moment for Saul as he examined his robe and saw the big piece missing from the hem.

"Saul, I don't understand why you've listened to those who have filled your ears with lies about my plans to harm you. Believe me, plenty of those who are with me would have been happy to help bring your life to an end. I almost had to physically restrain some of them. I told them you were the one God had anointed as our king. For some reason, you have yielded to the evil inside you and to the hotheads who surround you. You pretend that I have done something to threaten your rule, but that's simply not true. I have never done a thing to harm you, but you keep trying to kill me.

"If I were to lift my hand against you, I would be guilty of the same evil that makes you want to kill me. I have placed myself in the Lord's hands. If I have done any wrong toward you, I trust God to judge me accordingly. But the same God in whom I put my trust will surely judge you, King Saul, for your murderous intentions. I have no more strength than a flea before all your armies, but I am trusting God to protect me, in spite of my weakness. Before it is too late, turn back to the God who chose you to be our

king and who still loves you and is ready to forgive you for your
evil actions" (2 Samuel 24:8-15, paraphrased).

From this and other encounters between David and Saul, we
find an important principle that guides the Christian's view toward those in governmental leadership:

> **Christian citizenship is based on love and respect toward those
> in power, balanced by courageous and emphatic warnings when
> they have done wrong.**

The New Testament Teachings on Respecting Governmental Leaders

One of the more explicit teachings regarding respect for leaders
comes from 1 Peter 2:13-17. The passage begins with the principle
that we are to submit ourselves to those in leadership, governmental and otherwise. It is possible for someone to despise his or her
leaders and still submit to them. But the more demanding part of
the teaching tells us that we are to respect and honor the leaders:
"Show proper respect to everyone: Love the brotherhood of believers, fear god, honor the king."

Titus 3:1-2 reinforces this point by expressing the idea of
being in subjection and being obedient, while being peaceable,
considerate, and humble toward everyone, especially toward governmental leaders. If the apostle Paul had simply directed us to be
respectful toward people in general, his readers might have
thought he did not include those horrible Roman authorities. Paul,
who had his share of unpleasant encounters with Roman officials,
called on the followers of Christ to treat those in power as Christ
had taught and had practiced himself. We are to be respectful and
loving, even when the officials behave like King Saul and do not
deserve our respect.

Palestine in Paul's day had a two-tier system of government.
Along with the Roman governors and military officers, the Jewish
authorities were allowed to exercise considerable civil authority.
Paul, like Jesus, had as many nasty experiences with the Jews as
with the Romans. One of these encounters, recorded in Acts 23,
showed the profound respect Paul was willing to extend toward

Senator Hatfield on respect toward government leaders

"With prayer goes a certain respect for those holding authority, mentioned by Paul and similarly by Peter (1 Peter 2:17). This respect, however, is rooted in the proper and intended mandate that should be sought by those who hold earthly authority. Often, the Christian may see this mandate far more clearly than the one in authority, and hold it up with greater seriousness. Such respect in no way prohibits criticism and rebuking of those individuals in their misuse of authority. John the Baptist and Christ, as well as the prophets, give us clear examples."[10]

rulers who acted despicably. Brought before the Inquisition of his day, the Sanhedrin, Paul asserted he had been faithful to God and to his godly conscience. This was apparently not the right thing to say to the head of the Sanhedrin, the high priest, who promptly ordered those nearby to hit Paul in the face.

Paul, a patient and forgiving person, got a bit angry at the rough treatment he had received. He called the high priest a "whitewashed wall," using language similar to that which Jesus used for the Jewish officials. Jesus had compared them to nicely painted graves filled with rotting bodies.

"Excuse me, Paul, you just told off the high priest, the most powerful Jewish official."

"Oh, I'm so sorry. I didn't realize he was the high priest. We all know about the passage in Exodus that instructs us not to curse the rulers. I was out of line. I will stand firmly in the defense of my behavior as a follower of Christ, but I will not knowingly disrespect our leaders."

New Testament Teachings on Challenging the Actions of Governmental Leaders

As part of Jesus' rebuke of James and John for their efforts to maneuver themselves into a place of privilege among the disciples,

Jesus spoke about the inappropriate exercise of power that prevailed in their culture. He talked about those who "lord it over" others because of the power they are given. He used the opportunity to call his disciples and all who would later follow him to adopt the way of servanthood, not the way of arrogance and arbitrariness. Jesus rejected the evil behavior of officials, even though he modeled respectful behavior toward them (Mark 10:41-45).

As Jesus sent the disciples out to minister, he cautioned them that they would experience serious persecution and predicted they would receive harsh treatment from the officials. Jesus chose not to answer his accusers in their bogus judicial procedures, but he promised that his followers would be given the appropriate thing to say when they were challenged for being true to their convictions. He advised them to be ready to defend themselves and to stand firm against those who would falsely accuse and betray them. Once again we are taught to be firm against unjust treatment, while being respectful of those acting wrongly toward us (Matthew 10:16-20; Luke 21:12-19).

During Jesus' active teaching ministry, he was cautioned that Herod was planning to kill him. The Pharisees delivered the warning, not because of concern for Jesus, but because they thought they could frighten him into backing away from the teaching that was upsetting them. Jesus had no intention of letting this threat deter him. "Go tell that fox," Jesus said, "I will drive out demons and heal people today and tomorrow, and on the third day I will reach my goal." His reference to the timing of events between his crucifixion and resurrection went completely over the Pharisees' heads. But by his words Jesus modeled a respectful attitude toward officials and a commitment to the work of the kingdom that did not cease when he was threatened.

MEET GREG PRICKETT

People call him "Your Honor" and rarely use his name, Greg Prickett, during his official duties. He wears the robe that symbolizes the respect given to his position as judge. Those in the courtroom rise when he enters the room. More so than governors, mayors, and legislators, he is placed on a pedestal. But those who know Greg realize that none of his life on a pedestal changes the way he sees himself as God's servant in the judicial world. He is very mindful of the apostle Paul's teaching, "Do not think of yourself more highly than you ought, but rather think of yourself with sober judgment, in accordance with the measure of faith God has given you" (Romans 12:3).

People give Judge Prickett respect, whether they want to or not, but unlike King Saul in the dark period of his life, Greg works hard at holding himself accountable to the high standards God has for public servants. Greg is very serious about achieving the highest levels of fairness in the court system he serves.

Like William Wilberforce and Mark Hatfield, Greg Prickett was not committed to the lordship of Christ when he began his career as a public prosecutor in Southern California. He professed faith in Christ as a child, but had not walked with the Lord through his adolescent and early adult years. A neighbor kept inviting him to her church, not telling him her father was the pastor, but assuring him he would like the church, Rose Drive Friends Church, and would appreciate the pastor's preaching. He began attending that church, liked the preaching, and his childhood prayer for salvation became an adult commitment to Christ. Then a series of health crises among his loved ones helped Greg see his need for spiritual healing. In close succession, his father-in-law, his mother, and his daughter became seriously ill. He realized his spiritual resources were inadequate to help him face these crises and provide help to his loved ones.

After Greg had prosecuted major criminal cases in the Los Angeles District Attorney's office for 12 years, one of his former supervisors recommended Greg for a judgeship in Orange County. Governor Pete Wilson appointed Greg to the bench. Near the end of the long process Greg attended a Promise Keepers convention and heard a challenge from Chuck Swindoll to base our judgments on biblical standards. At about the same time, Greg's pastor, C.W. Perry, asked the people at Rose Drive Friends if they were more interested in their titles than in their testimony. Greg committed himself to use his judgeship for God's glory and as a means of witnessing to Christ's love and justice in his own life.

Judge Prickett now serves as superior court judge in Orange County and handles major felony cases, including rapes and murders. One of the ways he holds himself to a high standard of justice and fairness is by giving very careful attention to the jury selection process. He spends much more time than is typical to instruct prospective jurors. He emphasizes the need to recognize prejudice that might distort their decisions as jurors. He challenges jurors to see beyond their opinions and biases to the exercise of justice.

In keeping with the challenge of his pastor, Greg has been willing to use the respect given to his position as a door for sharing his faith in Christ. He has given his testimony at numerous prayer breakfasts and public gatherings. As lay pastor of missions in his church and chair of his denomination's mission board, Greg has visited mission work in numerous countries. He is delighted when the respect extended to a judge gives him the opportunity to talk about Christ. On one of these mission visits, a public official in Nepal was intrigued that a judge would be visiting his country and called on Greg to speak. Expecting a commentary on the court system in the United States, the man instead heard a forthright testimony about Greg's dependence on God for his work in the courts.

One of Judge Prickett's career theme verses has been Micah 6:8, "He has showed you, O man, what is good. And what does the Lord require of you? To act justly and to love mercy and to walk humbly with your God." He makes every effort to use his position of influence in the court system to assure that those who normally have no power in the government—widows, orphans, aliens, and prisoners—are treated with respect and fairness. His commitment to mercy does not make him withhold punishment from the guilty, but causes him to administer the penalty in a way that might bring the offender to a point of contrition for the crimes.

Storms

Storms that roil the sea and rake the land
are wonderful to watch if comfortably
ensconced at home, but burdensome
to workers who must cope with wind
and rain to fix the phones, remove debris.
Actually, such storms exhilarate.
They test our competence to cope.
More difficult to handle are the storms
that roil the mind and rake the soul.
Jealousy can generate a boiling surf
and tempests over turf can saturate
the social soil until edifices crumble.
Winds of carping criticism can chill
the wish to serve; they shrivel hope.
Maybe it's good to have some storms
that roil the sea and rake the land.
They let us reach outside ourselves
to embrace the needs of others,
and so fulfill the law of love.[11]
— *Arthur O. Roberts*

CHAPTER FOUR

Cheerfully Giving
Our Taxes

I parked my pickup truck and walked into my tax preparer's office. It was mid-February and I had gathered up all the W-2s, the 1099s, and the records of charitable giving and other deductible expenses. I had thought about the linkage between the Bible's teaching about cheerful giving with the teaching about paying our taxes. Based on the idea that my taxes can be a means of carrying out God's work, I should have been whistling cheerfully as I went into the tax preparer's office. It should have felt as good to pay taxes as it does to write out monthly checks to various Christian ministries. But I couldn't seem to help myself. I was not whistling. I felt nervous and discouraged about the checks I might have to write to the IRS and the Oregon tax office. Nothing about my manner in the meeting with the tax preparer that morning would have convinced him that I was a cheerful giver of my taxes.

Some sincere Christians have developed legal arguments for the proposition that it is unconstitutional and wrong to pay taxes. Others have knowingly manipulated their tax information to reduce their payments, feeling their excessive tax burden justifies their efforts to reduce their tax payments. How can these positions be grounded in a careful reading of the Bible? I observe that:

The Bible clearly and forcefully teaches us to give our taxes willingly, even though we may have legitimate questions about the wise use of these funds. The Bible also

suggests that we should give our taxes cheerfully, not grudgingly.

The Pharisees had mastered the art of entrapment. They were trained in theology and law. They lay awake at night thinking about questions they could ask Jesus that might undermine the consistency and validity of his teaching. Their favorite kind of trap raised doubts about Jesus' loyalty to God or to some other accepted authority. One day some Pharisees were only half listening to Jesus' parable about a wedding banquet. One of the Pharisees caught the eye of another Pharisee and indicated by his expression that he had just come up with a great question that would put Jesus in an awkward spot, maybe even discredit him among his listeners. The Pharisee preceded his question with flattery, calling Jesus a man of integrity, a great teacher of truth, and a careful discerner of people's worth. The Pharisee's insincerity was so painfully obvious one could almost hear people in the crowd saying, "Look out for this guy, Jesus. You know he doesn't believe an ounce of what he just said."

"Jesus, considering that you are a person of such high principles and seek to be completely consistent in your behavior, what is your instruction about paying the Roman taxes? You probably don't have a very high regard for the Roman government, so what is your advice about paying taxes to Caesar?"

The mumbling in the crowd began again, as Jesus paused to look at his questioner. Some thought this was the ultimate trap from which Jesus could not escape. They thought he might just walk away and not answer, since it was so obvious the Pharisee was not seeking spiritual and political advice. A few of Jesus' followers had heard an earlier exchange between Jesus and Peter about the temple taxes. The temple payments, administered not by the Romans but by the Jewish authorities, were obligatory, nothing like tithes and offerings. Jesus directed his disciples to go ahead and pay the temple tax as a witness of loyalty and duty and to avoid antagonism with those who collected the taxes. Jesus implied they would have a case for claiming exemption from the taxes as those who were being obedient to God's new order, not the old, worn-out Jewish legalism. But Jesus not only affirmed Peter's intention of paying the tax, he also performed an intriguing miracle of finding the tax money in a fish (Matthew 17:24-27).

Jesus' dialogue with the Pharisee about taxation took on a tone very different from the discussion with Peter. After pausing to reflect on the Pharisee's intentions, Jesus gave the questioner and his cohorts the name they fully deserved, "hypocrites." Jesus was always gentle and loving with those who came to God in sincere repentance and obedience. In fact, he had just recently talked about the warm welcome tax collectors would receive as they entered the Kingdom of God, repenting of their dishonest and burdensome ways of collecting taxes. He put them in the same category as prostitutes. This association would not have pleased them, but Jesus made it clear the Father was ready to receive anyone who came with a repentant spirit, however distasteful their conduct (Matthew 21:31-32).

Jesus told the Pharisees that the tax collectors and prostitutes would find their way into God's kingdom ahead of the Jewish authorities. That was a terrible thing for the religious leaders to hear. Then to be called hypocrites and masters of entrapment for asking the question about paying taxes felt horrible as well. But Jesus did more that day than expose the insincerity of the Jewish leaders; he took the opportunity to present one of his major teachings about active Christian citizenship. Without a moment's hesitation, he said his followers were to pay their taxes to the government, even though they knew how corrupt the Roman government was. He counseled his listeners to go beyond the level of duty and legalism. He used the verb *give* for the turning over of both the government taxes and the gifts to God's work (Matthew 22:15-22).

Jesus presented a revolutionary teaching that day in Jerusalem. He taught that his followers are to give willingly and cheerfully of their money and possessions, not just to God's work, but to the civil authorities, who also had the potential to do God's work.

A hush fell on the crowd that day as Jesus' listeners pondered this unconventional teaching. Some of his followers turned to each other and asked, "Did Jesus really mean to say we are to willingly pay taxes to Caesar, or was he just caught in another of the Pharisees' traps?" Peter heard one of these questions and answered, "No, Jesus has not been tricked. His words fit exactly with his teaching on the temple tax, that God's followers should not claim an exemption from what they are expected to give for public services. Yes, the Pharisee meant to entrap Jesus, but instead he gave Jesus the perfect chance to present one of the mysteries of the Kingdom of God. Jesus asserted that we have a dual citizenship with the heavenly and earthly kingdoms. I don't understand what that means, but Jesus made the tax part of it crystal clear. It's not exactly what we wanted to hear, but I don't expect the Master to change his mind on this issue."

While the crowd pondered Jesus' teaching, the Pharisees had their own discussion. They walked some distance away to get out of hearing range of the followers of Jesus. "I can't believe how he got out of that one," said one of the Pharisees. "Yes," said the one who had asked the question. "I had been thinking about that question for days. Just as Jesus finished the wedding story, it came to me how to ask it. I thought for sure he would say God's followers were only to give to God's work, not to the government. Had he done that we could have brought him before the Roman authorities today and charged him with disloyalty and sedition. Not only did Jesus say his followers were to pay their taxes, but he implied that they should do it with the same generous spirit in which they give to God's work. That's unbelievable. This guy is good. It will take a lot more than clever questions to make a case against him as a threat to the public order. We have some serious work to do." (See Matthew 22:22.)

Before his conversion, Paul might have asked similar questions about paying taxes. Paul came to understand that we are not

Senator Hatfield on paying taxes

"The principle of paying taxes is clearly accepted by the New Testament, for the government has valid and important functions to perform. However, whether specific portions of tax might be withheld from the government for activities which the Christian cannot condone could still be an open question not totally answered from Scripture; either side of such an argument could offer strong points from the Bible and Church history."[12]

only to pay our taxes out of duty and loyalty, but also to cheerfully make them available for important good work, just as we cheerfully give our tithes and offerings. This is one of the overlooked themes of Romans 13. The passage talks about public officials being God's servants, punishing wrongdoers when necessary, but primarily doing good things for the people they serve. Leaving no doubt about the importance of paying taxes, the passage says taxes are paid to enable officials to function as God's servants, to give their full attention to doing good. The passage leaves no room for grumbling about paying taxes; in fact it uses the verb *give*, just as Jesus did, suggesting the cheerful sharing of our resources for God's work in the public arena (Romans 13:1-7).

Cheerfulness about sharing our material resources is a theme Paul discussed a number of times in his writings. One of the strongest passages on this theme, 2 Corinthians 9, might logically apply to sharing our resources with the government as well as contributing to the Lord's work. "Each man should give what he has decided in his heart to give," says Paul, "not reluctantly or under compulsion, for God loves a cheerful giver" (2 Corinthians 9:6-8). Of course taxpayers do not have a choice of how much to give, which takes some of the joy out of the process, but the "cheerful giver" phrase fits very closely with Paul's teaching about taxes in Romans 13.

I was talking with a friend about the idea of cheerfully giving one's taxes and she said that was not a stretch at all for her. She told me about her grandson, who has a severe case of cerebral palsy. Sustaining his life has involved huge medical costs, incredibly expensive equipment and supplies, and skilled care. "My husband and I have paid a lot in taxes during our careers," she said, "but this has only been a small fraction of what has been provided for our grandson through various public assistance programs. God has taught us a lot about gratefully receiving help and cheerfully paying our taxes to help with the needs of others."

The Scripture passages we have considered provide us with a set of principles for the part of Christian citizenship that involves paying our taxes:

✓ Taxes are the means of carrying God's love to those in need, and Christians are taught to pay their taxes willingly and cheerfully.

✓ Paying our taxes is not a substitute for giving freely to Christian ministries of various kinds.

✓ Our objections to various governmental programs do not give us a reason to withhold our taxes or to grudgingly pay our taxes.[13]

✓ Christian citizens are to express their concerns to public officials about wasteful and inappropriate uses of tax money.

✓ We may feel that our total tax burden is heavy, but that does not justify finding illegal and inappropriate ways to reduce our taxes.

"Publican" was the polite name for these people in the days of Jesus. Their job, collection of Roman taxes, and their dishonest and unfair tactics in collecting the taxes made the Jews consider their vocation the lowest of the low. One of my neighbors has devoted his entire career to collecting taxes, but he does not bear much resemblance to the publicans of Jesus' day. Instead of using his position to enrich himself at the taxpayers' expense, he has given his energies to doing everything he can to make sure the federal tax laws are enforced fairly and carefully.

MEET RON GIEBENHAIN

His name is Ron Giebenhain. Even though most American taxpayers accept the idea of paying taxes, a few make mistakes, and some cut corners here and there, hoping they will not be caught. To hold taxpayers accountable, the Internal Revenue Service hires auditors, whose job it is to spot tax returns that might contain mistakes or even fraud. Often that results in more taxes, but sometimes auditors find that a taxpayer has a larger refund than expected.

Ron enjoys his restored Minneapolis Moline tractors and games of "pickle ball" in the recreation building on his farm near Newberg, Oregon. His pleasant manner does not square well with the negative stereotype of the tax auditor. Thirty years of auditing tax returns and training new IRS auditors may seem like an unpleasant career, but Ron enjoyed it. Realizing the fears a routine audit might generate, he made a point of putting himself in the taxpayer's position. "How would I like to be treated, if I were being audited?" Ron regularly asked himself. He began thinking not only about the taxpayer but also about the dozens of people with whom the taxpayer would talk about the audit experience. A negative account of a difficult experience could be repeated over and over again. On the other hand, setting the person at ease, answering questions, and showing the way to calculate the taxes accurately might result in positive stories about the IRS staff.

Ron realizes that some people dislike the IRS, forgetting that Congress writes the tax laws, not the tax agents. Complicated tax laws cause confusion and mistakes in filing tax returns, but the laws are meant to distribute the tax burden to accomplish specific national priorities. As attractive as it might seem to replace the complicated tax code with a "flat tax," Ron realizes that a flat tax would be burdensome to low income people and would benefit those who can afford to pay a greater share of their income for important public programs.

Is collecting taxes an honorable profession? Ron Giebenhain has no regret about his chosen vocation. An honorable profession? What a shock it must have been when Jesus began selecting his closest followers. Some wondered whether fishermen were suitable company for Jesus. Then Jesus spotted a man named Matthew, also called Levi. His vocation made him one of the most hated people of his day; he was a tax collector. Jesus asked him to become one of his followers and without hesitation Matthew agreed. Then when Matthew threw a party to celebrate his new association with Jesus, naturally some other tax collectors showed up. The "holier than thou" religious crowd thought Jesus should have nothing to do with these terrible people. Jesus said he liked them. They didn't spend a lot of time trying to impress others; they were willing to think about what Jesus said. The conversation at dinner might well have dealt with the ways tax collectors could carry out their work with justice and fairness. Matthew left his tax career behind when Jesus called him to be a disciple but his guests that day most likely continued in their tax work. And from that time they might have begun to do their jobs with a new ethic of honesty and fairness.

Ron Giebenhain is no longer an IRS auditor. He now is on the other side of the process as a CPA and tax preparer. He helps taxpayers deal with their complicated forms. When he talks about how the IRS might handle a particular issue in a tax return, he knows what he is saying. He has been there. And his manner makes it easier for a frustrated taxpayer to become a cheerful giver of taxes.

Leaner Not Meaner
The month of April makes clear
What our social contract costs.
Typically we grumble about
forms to be filled out and mailed,
along with hefty checks, to state
and federal tax collectors.
Our complaints are muted, though,
upon pondering the alternatives
to this democratic process.
Then we're of a mind to accept
(not too placidly, of course)
the bureaucratic procedures
required by a government
of, by, and for the people;
and we rejoice in covenants
solemnly fulfilled and paid for,
bringing freedom for others
as well as for ourselves.
We just want our government
to be leaner, not meaner,
so that it will be healthy,
and not perish from the earth.[14]
—Arthur O. Roberts

CHAPTER FIVE

Truthfulness in Public Service

I remember hearing, during my younger years, the story of Absalom getting his hair caught in an oak tree while his mule went on its way, leaving him hanging there. I cannot for the life of me think what we were supposed to learn from the story. Was it something about not letting your hair get too long? Or about the dangers of letting your mule go under trees? Or was it about the perils of getting out of hearing distance from your fellow soldiers? I had good teachers in Sunday school and vacation Bible school, so I'm sure there was something important we were supposed to learn from the story, but it escaped me.

The 2 Samuel passage about Absalom points to some important political lessons about truthfulness, lessons that relate directly to the responsibility of Christians to be active citizens. Like many of the Old Testament stories, the lesson comes from people who showed us how **not** to do something. Absalom's life was filled with tragedies he brought on himself because he did not have the strength of character to be truthful. His story could be the plot of a soap opera, with episodes of seduction, rape, murder, conspiracy, and political rebellion. It all ended in Absalom's humiliating execution while his hair was stuck in the oak tree's branches.

Absalom's father, King David, had many fine qualities and we are indebted to him for some wonderful parts of the Bible. But of course David's life was filled with tragic choices as well as heroic ones. We look at his life and see a lot that we should **not** do, as well as some positive models for righteous behavior.

David experienced terrible consequences as a result of his foolish adultery with Bathsheba and the arranged death of her husband, Uriah. One of the consequences of David's sinful behavior was the death of the son born to Bathsheba. The family problems in which Absalom figured may have also been among the further consequences of a king who chose short-term pleasure over moral restraint. David had children from at least six wives. Polygamy was common at the time, especially among the wealthy and powerful, and Scripture expresses no condemnation of David for having so many wives. But the Bible tells us about some terrible behavior among the siblings and half-siblings in his extended family.

Absalom's half-brother, Amnon, unwisely decided to pursue his romantic attraction to his half sister, Tamar. In the context it might appear that Amnon could have married Tamar if he had approached it appropriately, although today we would call this incest. In any event, Amnon did not handle his lust for Tamar appropriately. With the cooperation of a very naïve King David, Amnon arranged for Tamar to come to him and serve bread to him as part of a plot arranged with the help of the king's nephew, Jonadab. The plot was more elaborate than the one arranged by Potiphar's wife in her attempt to seduce Joseph, and the outcome was tragically different. Joseph escaped, but ended up in jail. Tamar was unable to talk Amnon out of having sex and was not physically strong enough to resist being raped by her half-brother (2 Samuel 13:1-21).

It seems that David should have figured out what Amnon had in mind, for Amnon's lust for Tamar had not been a secret in the king's household. As soon as Absalom saw Tamar with ashes on her head and with torn clothes, he guessed what had happened. Of course Absalom was very angry at what his half-brother

William Wilberforce on human evil

"Most educated, professing Christians either overlook or deny the corruption and weakness of human nature. They acknowledge there is, and always has been, a great deal of vice and wickedness. They recognize that mankind always has been prone to sensuality and selfishness, and therefore is disobedient to the more refined and liberal principles of their nature.

"These educated people can cite from all ages and cultures innumerable instances of oppression, rapacity, cruelty, fraud, envy, and malice; and they cite such occurrences in both public and private life. They acknowledge that it is in vain, too often, to inform those who thus misunderstand and to convince them about judgment. They admit that you do not thus reform the hearts of men.

"Although they know their duty, they will not practice it. No, they will not, even when they are forced to acknowledge that the path of virtue is also that of real interest and solid enjoyment."[15]

had done and King David was furious as well. But for the time being, Amnon was not punished for the abuse of his half-sister.

Many times as we read a story like the one about Amnon, Tamar, and Absalom, we hope that the "bad guy" will suffer as much as the person he has wronged. Since Absalom took it on himself to punish Amnon, we might think of him as the hero of this ugly episode. But this is not the lesson we ought to get from the passage. Absalom took advantage of the annual sheep-shearing gathering to carry out revenge on Amnon. The sheep-shearing event must have been like our modern hunting trips. Sheep shearing was not the real point of it; the hidden agenda was to drink and have a good time. After all, it was the servants who sheared the sheep, not the king's sons. But the event provided an excuse to get Amnon out of the king's palace. Again, the king was terribly naïve, not apparently understanding there was a reason Absalom was so eager for Amnon to join the sheep-shearing party. Actually, Absalom invited the king as well, but was not disappointed when David declined. It would have been messy to have his father present when the act of revenge was carried out.

Once Amnon joined the party, it was easy to carry out the murder plot. Absalom made sure Amnon had plenty to drink and Amnon did not even put up a struggle. Did Amnon deserve being murdered for the sin of rape? According to Hebrew laws, probably so. Did Absalom have the right to carry this out himself, with no "due process" according to Jewish law and no consent from the king? No. This is where the story gets more interesting and relates more directly to the theme of truthfulness in the political setting. After the murder, Absalom's other half-brothers lost no time in jumping on their mules and heading in every direction. They had no interest in getting blamed for Amnon's killing, for they knew how their father felt about revenge and murder. This was apparent from David's unwillingness to kill King Saul and his anger at the person who took Saul's life.

Long before Absalom's half-brothers had the courage to show up at the king's palace, a report got back to David that Absalom had killed not just Amnon, but all the other sons of the king as well. What could have been the source of this rumor? Would the king's servants have gone back to the palace with a false report, intending to make the king more distressed than he would have been with the death of Amnon alone? They had no reason to do that. Absalom might have been responsible for the rumor, for he had little concern for his father's feelings. He might have hoped his father would be so relieved when he learned his sons were alive that he would forget about being angry with Absalom for carrying out "justice" in such an inappropriate way.

David's commander in chief, Joab, was not sure whether Absalom would be safe in returning to the palace and set about to test the king's feelings. Joab sent a woman to David to tell a story about sibling rivalry and murder. Nathan had used similar tactics when he exposed the king's wrongdoing with Bathsheba. But in this case the king's sin was not at issue but what David might do about Absalom's sin. David was naïve at times, but he was not stupid. He realized Joab had sent the woman. David made it clear that he would not harm Absalom, but in this case it was Joab who was naïve, thinking Absalom would repent of his murder and deception (2 Samuel 14:1-22).

One might have expected David to act like the father in the New Testament story of the prodigal son. But David did an interesting thing when Absalom came back to town. David said he would not harm his son, but did not allow Absalom to come to the palace and pretend that nothing had happened. David could have extended God's forgiveness to Absalom without condoning the sibling revenge and murder. But here we see a less naïve side of David. We see David acting on the assumption that Absalom was not a person to be trusted, that the murder of Amnon was only the beginning of a pattern of lying and rebellion.

Absalom himself ended the awkward alienation with his father. One would wish that this happened as a result of Absalom's repentant and humble spirit, but this was not the case. Absalom asked Joab to arrange a meeting with his father, but Joab refused. Absalom tried again and Joab refused to even talk with him. Revealing the dark side of his character, Absalom then had his servants set one of Joab's fields on fire to get his attention. These crude tactics finally worked and the two met and arranged a meeting with the king. Humility was evident in the interaction of David and Absalom, but Absalom did not acknowledge he had offended his father and God by killing his brother. David kissed his son, but there was no further expression of genuine reconciliation and repentance (2 Samuel 14:25-33).

Absalom's pattern of deception and conspiracy escalated to a new level after the meeting with his father. Knowing that people from the kingdom would go to the city gates to seek help from the king and his staff with their disputes and questions, Absalom began going each day to a place on the road to the city gates. There he established himself and his entourage so he could talk with people before they got to the city. Using rhetoric and tactics strikingly like modern political campaigns, Absalom spoke negatively about the king and his officials. He assured people that if he were in a key position of leadership, he would be able to take care of all their needs. His glib promises, his good looks, and his phony affection won him many friends. Word spread rapidly that he was a person to be considered for future national leadership (2 Samuel 15:1-8).

From deceit and conspiracy, Absalom moved quickly into open rebellion. David continued to trust his son and gave his blessing for Absalom to go to Hebron and fulfill a vow to worship there. But David could no longer overlook Absalom's rebellion, for Absalom convinced his followers to proclaim him king. David immediately capitulated, left his palace and Jerusalem unguarded, and fled to the countryside with those of his subjects who were still loyal. The story in 2 Samuel continues with great detail as the rebellion expanded into civil war, and plotting and spying continued between rebels and loyalists.

The climactic battle of the rebellion had an amazing and very sad outcome for Absalom, the rebel leader. David had wanted to join the battle with his own troops, but his generals convinced him that if any harm came to him, the loyalist cause would be doomed. David conceded, but cautioned his troops that they must not harm his son Absalom. The battle did not go well for Absalom's rebels, fighting in the forest of Ephraim. Absalom lost 20,000 warriors in one day. Amazingly, in the confusion of the horrible battle Absalom was separated from his men. Then his mule did what any mule would do to bring an end to its part in the battle. The phrase "stubborn as a mule" probably has a counterpart in the Hebrew language, for the mule headed straight for a thick oak tree, hoping to dislodge its rider. The plan of the rebellious mule worked perfectly and became the turning point of the entire battle. Instead of rallying his troops to retake the lead in the battle, Absa-

Senator Hatfield on the truthfulness of public officials

"In the minds of most people there is a latent suspicion that politicians are somehow dishonest or at least very flexible ethically. Reports of the misconduct of public officials, which always receive front-page attention in the newspapers, serve to support the popular notion that all office holders are less than completely honest if not just plain crooked. Disclosures of influence peddling, misuse of funds, and falsifying government pay records by trusted public servants cause great damage to the people's trust of government officials.

"Our newspaper headlines give us new reasons to suspect that few public office holders are honest. We are stunned to hear a sub-cabinet official state that the government has the right to lie to the people. We hear constantly of the 'credibility gap' in government—the distance between the truth and what is told to the nation. Influence peddling and fraud by government employees and their friends cause us to wonder what has become of integrity in public service."[16]

lom was left hanging by his hair in the tree, while the mule headed for a safe place. For some reason, none of Absalom's men could hear his shouts for help, but his shouts did attract the attention of the loyalist troops.

Seeing Absalom's predicament but remembering their king's stern command to do no harm to his son, one of the soldiers went to report the situation to Joab, David's commander in chief. Joab had learned how to manipulate his boss and decided to ignore the command to protect Absalom. Joab and his soldiers killed Absalom, ending the rebellion. One of Joab's men, Ahimaaz, wanted to carry the word to the king about Absalom's death, but Joab knew the one carrying the message could be at considerable risk. So Joab sent a Cushite with the message; Cushites were expendable. Apparently Ahimaaz had visions of winning an Olympic marathon medal, for he begged to run to the king with the message, even after the Cushite runner left. Ahimaaz won the race, but did not have the courage to deliver the message to the king. He knew that good news for the kingdom was bad news for its king, who had just lost a son he loved very much. The Cushite was willing to tell David of his son's fate and fortunately for the Cushite, David's reaction was remorse for his son, not anger at the messenger.

After hearing of his son's death David bitterly repeated the phrase "O my son Absalom," an epitaph for a young man whose motto was "the end justifies the means." Absalom pioneered the ethics later advocated by the sixteenth-century Italian political philosopher Niccolo Machiavelli, who condoned deception, disloyalty, and violence if it benefited the politician.

David's life was a mixture of tragedy and triumph. He was to blame for the tragic seduction of Bathsheba and the murder of Uriah. David was not responsible for Absalom's deception and rebellion, but he should have been more willing to deal with his son's treasonous conduct. If David had followed the principles in one of his own great poems, things might have gone better for him and Absalom might have been spared such a humiliating end. Psalm 101:3-8 expresses the duty of a king to confront evildoers, advice that David chose to ignore in the case of his son Absalom:

> The deeds of faithless men I hate; they will not cling to me.
> Men of perverse heart shall be far from me;
> I will have nothing to do with evil.
> Whoever slanders his neighbor in secret, him will I put to silence;
> whoever has haughty eyes and a proud heart, him will I not endure.
> My eyes will be on the faithful in the land, that they may dwell with me;
> he whose walk is blameless will minister to me.
> No one who practices deceit will dwell in my house;
> no one who speaks falsely will stand in my presence.
> Every morning I will put to silence all the wicked in the land;
> I will cut off every evildoer from the city of the Lord.

Time after time the Bible teaches that truthfulness is expected of those who are serious followers of God. In Zechariah 8:16-17, we read, "'These are the things you are to do: Speak the truth to each other, and render true and sound judgment in your courts; do not plot evil against your neighbor, and do not love to swear falsely. I hate all this,' declares the Lord." The apostle Paul quoted a passage from Psalm 5 that demonstrated human sinfulness. Part of this description dealt with the prevalence of dishonesty, "Their throats are open graves; their tongues practice deceit. The poison of vipers is on their lips. Their mouths are full of cursing and bitterness" (Romans 3:13-14).

Anyone who has been close to government officials is aware there are those who are willing to be dishonest or to be selective about the truth for their own self-protection and the advancement of their own causes. Governments are not filled with liars as some might assume, but complete truthfulness is an unusual trait. The problem may be connected with the fact that a considerable number of people in elective and appointive office in the United States are trained as lawyers. Practicing law requires one to provide the best possible defense for a client. It involves presenting an account of events that might not be true but might be plausible. If there is falsehood in the lawyer's presentation, it is up to the opposing attorney to bring this to light and for the judge and jury to discern truth from fabrication. This approach can find its way into political rhetoric and tactics. Officials and citizens committed to following God's truth are not given the option of being deceitful to further their causes. There is no room for Absaloms among godly citizens.

The following principles summarize the biblical case for truthfulness as it applies to active citizenship:

✓ There is no place for lying and deceit in the life and work of officials and citizens.

✓ Being known for truthfulness can be an asset in politics. When a person carries out his or her promises and does not hide the truth, public trust can result. Good news can sometimes travel fast.

✓ Surrounded by people who believe that the end justifies the means, one must choose to forego deceitful shortcuts to political accomplishments.

✓ Politicians and citizens sometimes engage in political struggles involving moral issues that may relate directly to Christian convictions. Even godly ends do not justify ungodly means.

✓ Dealing with people on a regular basis who have no problem with being untruthful can weaken the resolve of a godly person in politics. One should seek out the fellowship and encouragement of those who recognize the necessity of being fully truthful.

MEET DENNIS GOECKS

Dennis Goecks looks back on his eight years as a county commissioner and recalls his contributions to the broader public good and to individuals as well. It feels good to him that the government of Yamhill County was able to serve the needs of its citizens while he was in office without increasing the relative size of its budget. Dennis feels even better about being able to help individuals like Johnny Kilmer, a gentleman with special needs who works at a sheltered workshop in the county. Johnny was grateful for the ways Dennis helped the agency that employed him and offered to help in Dennis's campaigns in return. Dennis feels one of the best things local government can do is help people find a way to support themselves and live a meaningful life.

Dennis is an example of people with careers outside government who step into the public arena to use their experience and training in active citizenship roles. He was talking with someone in his church one day about the need for Christians to become more active in applying their convictions in public service. That friend suggested he consider practicing what he was preaching. After some thought and prayer, Dennis did that. He was defeated in his first campaign, then won two elections and served two terms of four years each. He was defeated by only eleven votes in his campaign for a third term.

The issue of truthfulness has been a source of both frustration and satisfaction for Dennis. He came from a business career in which speaking forthrightly and honestly was essential, but he was appalled at the lack of truthfulness in local politics. He felt that journalists sometimes misrepresented what he had said and done in order to satisfy the public appetite for controversy. He felt that his opponents along the way were willing to shade the truth to enhance their chances of being elected or to support their side of a policy debate. At times he compared himself to a volunteer sitting on the platform of a dunk tank, inviting people to take aim and send him into the cold water. He felt his oath of office bound him to be true to the law, to be truthful in expressing his positions, and to be fair and honest in talking about his opponents.

Dennis has some advice for those who might be considering running for public office:

✓ Count the cost in advance, in terms of the time demands, the emotional pressure, and the loss of personal privacy for self and family.

✓ Make sure one's relationship with God is strong and that one has a healthy prayer life.

✓ Know that there are rewards and satisfactions that are greater than the proposals and policies that get adopted.

CHAPTER SIX

Government as an Instrument of Compassion

"Bill, I've decided to stop taking the newspaper. I get so frustrated reading the news about the latest events in Washington. Congress meets around the clock sometimes, just thinking of ways to spend more of our money. Every once in a while I read about some member of Congress with the courage to blow the whistle on all the government waste. They find examples of the government spending $90,000 for a study of why hummingbirds have long beaks. That may be a slight exaggeration, but actually I hear many examples of Congress wasting our money and their time on such things. I wonder if governments have ever limited themselves to doing good things for people, things they really need."

"Ted, I can identify with your frustration. I get pretty weary of that sort of thing myself, even though I feel our governments do many good things. I just wish our politicians could tell the difference between meeting human needs and doling out money for ridiculous and unnecessary projects. But your comments brought to mind our Sunday school class; we have been studying the life of Joseph. I knew all the stories about his dreams as a young teenager, his brother's hatred and jealousy, his near death at their hands, his sale into slavery, and the tough times he had as a young man. He tried to be true to God while surrounded by paganism and ruthless behavior. But in the last couple of weeks we got to the part that connects with what you're saying. Why don't you signal the waitress to refill our coffee cups and I'll give you a few thoughts about Joseph's adult years as a national leader? It seems to me he is the prime example of guiding a government toward the careful use of resources to meet human needs."

Joseph may have wished at times that God had not gifted him with the ability to interpret dreams. When as a boy he told about his dreams of sheaves of grain and the heavenly bodies bowing down before him, he found himself in deep trouble. In fact, his brothers tossed him into a deep cistern. The smart advice to Joseph would have been to keep the dreams to himself. In his immaturity he blurted out the dreams and the idea of bowing down before him did not amuse his brothers.

Skipping ahead from Joseph's first dream experience, his next encounter with dreams involved his fellow inmates, Pharaoh's cupbearer and baker. Joseph's interpretation of the cup-bearer's dream contained good news—in three days he would be released from prison and restored to his position in the king's household. The baker's dream indicated the opposite outcome. The cupbearer did get his job back and the baker was executed. The baker had no chance to blame Joseph for the awful dream and, unfortunately, the cupbearer forgot Joseph's request that he ask Pharaoh to release him from jail.

The third of Joseph's dream experiences speaks directly to the idea of governments as agents of God's compassion toward human need. Like the previous dreams this one came in a pair. Knowing the rest of the story, we may find it puzzling that all Pharaoh's political advisors and philosophers could not figure out the meaning of the simple dreams. Seven skinny cows ate up seven fat cows and seven skinny stalks of grain ate up seven healthy stalks of grain. But without having read the Genesis story many times, maybe we would not find it so easy to translate the dreams into seven years of bountiful harvests and seven years of drought (Genesis 41).

Senator Mark Hatfield on compassionate government

"If Christians in political life cannot be witnesses in this most basic manifestation of the living Word on a day-to-day basis, then the whole concept of public service is a mockery. Of course, I often fail in this area. But it is a deep desire of my heart to be a reflection, however pale, of the Incarnate One who encountered the destitute widow of Nain in her need and who fed the hungry multitudes. It has become increasingly obvious to me that Christians reaching out in deed as well as word to touch the lives of the poor, the oppressed, the lonely, and the frightened, are the only expression in the flesh of the living Christ that many people are going to know. Wilberforce was certain, as I am, that social progress, if it is to be true, needs a biblical base."[17]

Fortunately for Pharaoh and for Joseph, the cupbearer overcame his memory loss and recalled that he knew about a person who was good at interpreting dreams, the young Hebrew falsely accused of seducing his master's wife. We can admire many things about Joseph. One of them was his emphatic trust in God and his willingness to make that clear to everyone. People assumed Joseph's own wisdom allowed him to interpret the cupbearer's and baker's dreams. But before he even heard about the contents of the dream, Joseph said he had no ability whatsoever to give an interpretation. Only if God chose to give the interpretation through him would anything useful be learned from the dream. The Genesis account does not indicate Pharaoh's reaction to Joseph's statement of trust in God, but later events show the king was impressed with the humility and courage of this young man.

If Joseph had been a political schemer, he might have made up the interpretation of the dream so Pharaoh would need the services of a good food administrator. But the idea that Joseph himself would be given the responsibility to deliver Egypt from disaster would have been mind-boggling. Imagine Joseph sitting in prison and saying to one of his fellow inmates that the next day he would be standing before Pharaoh interpreting a dream and moments later would become the most powerful administrator in the government. Does one hear loud laughter in the background?

In addition to interpreting the dreams, Joseph went on to say that the only way to avert national disaster was to find someone who understood the situation and was a strong leader. The person must be able to develop a food storage program sufficient to meet the needs of Egypt and surrounding nations during a terrible drought. A younger Joseph might have gone on to say, "By the way, Pharaoh, in case you can't think of someone who would do a good job with this assignment, I'm available." Joseph had matured and he left it to Pharaoh to think of him as the person to make the plan work.

Pharaoh's advisors had not done so well in interpreting the king's dream. They also were tongue-tied when he asked them if they could think of a good food administrator. Maybe it was the special requirement Pharaoh placed in the job description. He said he needed someone whose thinking and work were guided by God. The officials scratched their heads and tried to think of people who had good track records as administrators and who knew about agriculture and the storage of agricultural commodities. As they huddled to come up with nominations, they thought of quite a few people with those skills.

Some of those in the king's court itself felt they could handle the assignment and thought it would be a great way to rise in power in the empire. But the more the officials talked, the more troubled they became about the spiritual qualifications. Pharaoh had said he needed someone filled with the spirit of God. If he had meant someone who knew all about the Egyptian gods, any of the nominees would have qualified. But it seemed from Pharaoh's dialogue with Joseph that he might have been talking about someone who knew how to draw on the wisdom and power of the Hebrew God, Jehovah. The Egyptian advisors knew something about this

William Wilberforce on compassion through government

"Take the example of lovingkindness and meekness toward others. Observe the solid foundation which self-denial, temperance, and humility lay for them. The chief causes of strife and enmity among men are pride and self-importance, and the consequent courtesies they demand from others. Other causes are the over-valuation of worldly possessions, world honor and, in consequence, a too eager competition for them. The rough edges of one man rub against those of another. The friction thus disturbs the just arrangement and regular motions of society. But Christianity files down all these roughnesses.

"But bless be God the real religion which we recommend has proved its consistency with the original character of Christianity, namely its concern for the poor. It has proved this by changing the whole condition of the mass of society in many of the most populous districts of this and other countries."[18]

God of the Hebrews, but they were not about to claim that they served Jehovah as their only god. That itself could have landed them in prison where Joseph had been. So the officials ended their huddle, looked at Pharaoh helplessly, and offered no nominations for "food czar" (Genesis 41:33-38).

During the caucus of the king's officials Joseph stood nearby, wondering if he was five minutes from being sent back to jail or if there was something more in his future. It was absurd to think that Pharaoh would pick him to run the food program. But the absurd happened that day in Pharaoh's palace. In one of the most dramatic political events in the entire Bible, Pharaoh turned in disgust from the blank looks on the faces of his officials and focused on Joseph. Yes, Joseph had spent some years in jail, not exactly a promising feature of his resume. But the open secret in the palace was that Joseph did not deserve his prison sentence. And without a doubt Joseph met the requirement none of the officials could fulfill, that the person be completely guided and controlled by the Spirit of God.

Not only did Pharaoh shock everyone that day, including Joseph, by appointing him as food administrator, but Pharaoh also gave him an instant promotion. He would become the second most powerful person in Egypt, in charge of all the king's work and overseeing all the king's officials. Who could think of a more dramatic "rags to riches" story than that of Joseph? One day stuck in jail; the next day running the country.

But the point of the story is not just that God can deliver one who is faithful to him. The story shows how Joseph set about to demonstrate the good things governments are able to do when God guides their work. What a huge task Joseph had. In spite of all the power he had been given, he had to run a food storage program that seemed completely unrealistic. The rationale for storing all the grain was based on Pharaoh's dream and its interpretation by a Hebrew slave and inmate. Think of all the income the Egyptians lost since they could not sell their surplus during the plentiful years. Think of all the expense of building facilities to keep the grain in good condition and secure from looting. Think of all the complaining from those who thought the whole idea was ridiculous, that the grain would just spoil and be eaten by rodents. The Egyptians could not be certain that years of drought lay ahead. Joseph had a hard job on his hands, but fortunately he remained focused on God's power at work in his life. Each time he and his wife were blessed with sons, Joseph pronounced a blessing, giving God all the credit for his own good circumstances and the success of his work (Genesis 41:50-52).

As hard as it had been to collect and store the grain in a fair and efficient way, the more difficult work began when the famine set in. Joseph had to plan carefully to ration the food so it would last for seven years. He had to be sure each storage facility was secure from those who would want to steal the grain and sell it on the black market. He had to decide how much grain could be sold to hungry people in neighboring countries without running out of food for the Egyptian people themselves. He had to keep his focus on the God who empowered and guided him, so his political clout did not distract him from faithfully carrying out God's work in this situation.

Many other dramatic events mark Joseph's life, including the incredible story of his reunion with his family. His family had joined the steady stream of pilgrims coming to Egypt to plead for food.

The central principles evident from leadership in the government of Egypt are these:

✓ God can use a government as an agent of preserving human life and ministering to human need.

✓ Essential for a government to become an instrument of compassion is the work of public officials who have the talent and courage to carry out programs that meet human needs.

✓ Only government can in certain situations carry out large-scale efforts to mobilize important resources for compassionate work.

✓ Christians should be very careful about adopting the ethos of their surrounding culture, which tends to be very negative about governments.

The New Testament writers did not have contemporary examples of governments that were devoted to doing good things for people and serving God's purposes. But the "political chapter" in the New Testament, Romans 13, is filled with the imagery of a government that does good work and public officials who are God's agents for doing good. For all the apostle Paul's knowledge of the Scriptures, it is surprising he did not refer to Joseph's leadership in Egypt when he talked about public officials as "God's servants." Three times in quick succession Paul used the servant phrase, indicating that the servant of God in the government was there to do good things, to punish wrongdoers, and to be fair and just administrators. Joseph had done all those things. Joseph, more than any other biblical figure, gives us the model of a good person doing good work through the government in a way that no person could do on his or her own.

MEET JEFF MERKLEY

He has had quite a variety of employers—the Department of Defense, the Congressional Budget Office, Habitat for Humanity, the World Bank, and the World Affairs Council of Oregon. He has now added to that varied career a period of service in the Oregon House of Representatives. He has studied complex weapons systems; he has been a provider of services to low income families. He now balances the work of educating the public about global issues with his involvement in a host of issues affecting the citizens of Oregon.

His name is Jeff Merkley and he grew up in the part of Portland, Oregon, he now represents in the legislature. With degrees from Stanford and Princeton, he has always been fascinated with the ways public policies are shaped. In the legislature, he finds it difficult to counter some of the forces that are determined to maintain the status quo. But he celebrates small political victories and keeps looking for ways to persuade other legislators to take his side on behalf of those who need the protection or the services of the government.

Jeff's issues of choice in politics are education, consumer rights, and the environment. He assumes that the wealthy and powerful in the state are able to present their case to the public and that he should advocate for those who are not normally heard. Like Senator Mark Hatfield, for whom Jeff once served as an intern, Jeff likes to calculate the human benefit if some of the funds from major weapons systems could be shifted to things such as providing small grants to families for purchasing their own home. He visualizes a future in which tens of millions of families could have good homes if just one of the major weapons systems were canceled. Also like Senator Hatfield, Jeff does not always stick with the predictable position of the social liberal. He has done battle with the state lottery program on the grounds that the poor are the most addicted to this form of gambling and have the least disposable resources for such forms of "recreation." As one of his small victories, he was responsible for the passage of a bill requiring that lottery advertising carry a disclaimer pointing out that lotteries are a form of recreation, not an investment.

Jeff speaks of living with one foot in the world of poverty and one foot in the world of power. That image connects with much of his life as he has worked with national and state policy formation in various ways but has always tried to understand the impact of the policy choices on the poor. Like Joseph in the Old Testament, Jeff realizes he has been blessed with a fine education and the opportunity to influence others. He hopes his work will be an expression of compassion and will have a broad benefit, as was the case with Joseph.

CHAPTER SEVEN

Government as an Instrument of Justice

"The Lord will guide you always; he will satisfy your needs in a sun-scorched land and will strengthen your frame. You will be like a well-watered garden, like a spring whose waters never fail. Your people will rebuild the ancient ruins and will raise up the age-old foundations; you will be called Repairer of Broken Walls, Restorer of streets with Dwellings" (Isaiah 58:11-12).

This wonderfully hopeful statement comes from one of the greatest biblical prophets. Who wouldn't want to be like a well-watered garden and an inexhaustible spring? And who wouldn't want to be known as a rebuilder, a repairer, and a restorer? But much more than beautiful literature, this passage, in its context, sheds light on one of the most important and least understood biblical concepts — justice. Time after time this word is used among Christians in a way that indicates they have little comprehension of what God meant us to understand about justice. Active Christian citizenship requires serious attention to the concept of justice.

The prophet Isaiah's ministry took place during events that ranged from bad to terrible. Isaiah's work began with a vision of angels purifying his tongue so he could deliver God's truth to a disobedient people. He asked how long the people would continue their stubborn inattentiveness to God's call to repentance.

The answer came: Their evil would continue until the land was destroyed and the people carried away into exile (Isaiah 6:8-13). This discouraging prediction was fulfilled almost immediately, as the Assyrian king Tiglath-Pileser carried off large numbers of the northern Hebrew kingdom of Israel, with its capital in Samaria. Not one king of Israel had been a godly spiritual leader and none had paid attention to God's warnings of punishment for national disobedience and evil.

The kingdom of Judah survived during the time of Isaiah's ministry, and parts of it were not completely defeated until more than a century later. It certainly helped that a few of the kings of Judah called their people back to worship Jehovah God. During Isaiah's time, Jotham was a good king and Hezekiah was a superb godly leader. In fact, Isaiah interrupted his general messages to the people to tell about Hezekiah's heroic resistance to the attack of Sennacherib, king of Assyria.

As Isaiah delivered his warnings, some of his listeners were repentant, but most paid as little attention as the people had to Noah's weather forecasts. The subject of this chapter, the meaning of justice in God's value system, was a theme of great importance for Isaiah and other prophets. The Scripture quotation at the beginning of this chapter only hints at the meaning of "justice" in the Bible. To get the point of Isaiah's proclamations about justice to the kings and people of his day skip over Isaiah 58 and note how Isaiah 59 vividly describes what justice is not. The chapter begins with a lament about the darkness of the conduct of a people who had consistently rebelled against God:

> Surely the arm of the Lord is not too short to save, nor his ear too dull to hear. But your iniquities have separated you from your God: your sins have hidden his face from you, so that he will not hear. For your hands are stained with blood, your fingers with guilt. Your lips have spoken lies, and your tongue mutters wicked things. (Isaiah 59:1-3)

Senator Mark Hatfield on Justice

"Deprivation, suffering, hunger, alienation from God and man, lack of dignity, oppression—these strangle the world's hope for true peace. These are the obstacles to peace. True, they are perpetrated by sin—the sin of those who, absorbed by their wealth, power, privilege, and supposed self-righteousness, are blind to the responsibility of meeting these needs. Such sin is too often our own.

"Christ calls us to witness to his life through our lives. That witness involves ministering to man whenever and wherever he is in need. One of the parables of our Lord provides us with valuable insights into our responsibilities as Christians. After Jesus told of the necessity to love one's neighbor, he was asked, 'Who is my neighbor?' Then followed the story of the Good Samaritan in which the victim was a complete stranger to those who passed by without stopping to help, as well as to the Samaritan. The persons in this story are not individually identified; there is no indication of who it was that was robbed and injured. The point is that one's neighbor is *anyone* in need. We cannot choose our charities. When confronted with simple human need, we are called to act—and to love. As we heal wounds, we nurture peace."[19]

Then Isaiah gets to the point of the chapter and repeats it so many times one would have to be blind to miss it:

✓ "No one calls for justice." (v. 4)

✓ "There is no justice in their paths." (v. 8)

✓ "Justice is far from us." (v. 9)

✓ "We look for justice, but find none." (v. 11)

✓ "Justice is driven back." (v. 14)

✓ "There was no justice." (v. 15)

Saying this six times in 15 verses certainly indicates its importance, but what exactly does he mean by "justice"? In Isaiah 59 we read about the violent oppression of innocent people and the complete abandonment of honesty and truth. But Isaiah 58 begins by expressing the wonder of the Hebrew people that they faithfully worshiped and served God, but God did not seem to notice. In fact, they not only kept the law, they practiced self-denial by fasting on a regular basis. What more could God want than people who were going out of their way to live holy lives? As a matter of fact, God wants much more than faithful worship.

As is later echoed in the book of James, Isaiah 58 says fasting means nothing unless it is associated with the just treatment of other people. Isaiah makes his meaning vividly clear; he describes injustice:

✓ The exploitation of workers. (v. 3)

✓ Quarreling and strife, resulting in physical violence. (v. 4)

✓ Oppressing people, treating them like animals put to work in the field. (v. 9)

✓ False accusations. (v. 9)

Isaiah also brings out the positive side of justice:

✓ Freeing those in human bondage. (v. 6)

✓ Providing food, shelter, and clothing for those in need. (v. 7)

Hold it, Isaiah. That's not much of a list! No, it's not a long list, but it provides a great place to begin. And in chapter 59, Isaiah does something very common in the Old Testament. Woven through the many references to justice are repeated mentions of the biblical concept of righteousness. Actually, the two terms are interchangeable. Isaiah said, "Justice is far from us, and righteousness does not reach us" (Isaiah 59:9). And again in the same chapter, he said, "Justice is driven back, and righteousness stands at a distance" (Isaiah 59:14). Righteousness is associated with the very essence of God and as we commit ourselves to God and begin to

William Wilberforce on the importance of justice

"Following peace with all men and looking upon them as members of the same family, entitled to justice and brotherly kindness, he would be respected and beloved by others. He would himself be free from the annoyance of those bad passions that are activated by worldly principles and are so commonly corrosive. If such men filled any country, each thus diligently discharging the duties of his own place in society without impinging the rights of others, then all the world indeed would be active and harmonious in the human family."[20]

live godly lives, we take on that character of righteousness. And we give evidence of that righteousness by the right treatment of God's creatures, our fellow humans.

Scattered through the other prophetic books are these passages that add to our understanding of biblical justice:

"'Administer true justice; show mercy and compassion to one another. Do not oppress the widow or the fatherless, the alien or the poor. In your hearts do not think evil of each other.'" (Zechariah 7:9-10)

"Listen, you leaders of Jacob, you rulers of the house of Israel. Should you not know justice, you who hate good and love evil; who tear the skin from my people and the flesh from their bones; who eat my people's flesh, strip off their skin and break their bones in pieces; who chop them up like meat for the pan, like flesh for the pot?" (Micah 3:1-3)

"For three sins of Israel, even for four, I will not turn back my wrath. They sell the righteous for silver, and the needy for a pair of sandals. They trample on the heads of the poor as upon the dust of the ground and deny justice to the oppressed." (Amos 2:6-7)

For I know how many are your offenses and how great your sins. You oppress the righteous and take bribes and you deprive the poor of justice in the courts. (Amos 5:12)

> Hear this, you who trample the needy and do away with the
> poor of the land, saying, "When will the New Moon be over
> that we may sell grain, and the Sabbath be ended that we may
> market wheat?" —skimping the measure, boosting the price
> and cheating with dishonest scales, buying the poor with silver
> and the needy for a pair of sandals, selling even the sweepings
> with the wheat. (Amos 8:4-6)

We could find many similar passages. This is not an obscure biblical teaching. But we confuse the issue by associating biblical justice with our contemporary ideas of just treatment by our governments, particularly in the courts. Actually the biblical and the contemporary definitions do overlap. Contemporary injustice looks much like the biblical examples—corrupt court systems, violent treatment of the innocent, neglect of the basic necessities of large segments of the population. But too often people think of justice as retribution for illegal and inhumane treatment of others. Justice is much more than that, at least in the biblical context.

Justice in the Bible means treating people as God's created beings, giving them a life free of oppression and exploitation. Justice and its synonym in the Bible, righteousness, mean acting as God's agents to treat people righteously, especially those with the greatest needs. Governments characterized by justice are those that treat the poor and powerless as full citizens in God's kingdom.

MEET ARTHUR ROBERTS

The prophet Isaiah spoke of those who work for justice as "repairers of broken walls" and "restorer of streets with dwellings." This prophetic vision of building communities shaped by just relationships motivated Arthur Roberts to relinquish some of the time he could have devoted to writing poetry and scholarly books. While a professor of philosophy at George Fox College (now University), he served on the local planning commission. He also ran, unsuccessfully, for the state legislature. Some of his students found it hard to grasp many of his ideas and vocabulary and were surprised that he became interested in public policy. He first got involved in some land development projects and learned that decisions in local government are sometimes made on the basis of backroom deals rather than in accordance with the spirit of the law.

When he and his wife, Fern, retired they bought a beach home in Yachats, an Oregon central coast town of seven hundred residents, whose major "industries" are retirement and tourism. He had writing projects to finish and he also wanted to stay in touch with colleagues at George Fox. This he did by writing several books, editing a theological journal, and teaching some classes. But even though many people thought of him as a man of ideas and abstractions, he felt he should begin serving his community. As Arthur and Fern got acquainted with people in Yachats, they realized there were many other well-educated people in the community. But many of them were unwilling to volunteer time and energy in preserving the beauty and the smooth operation of the city. Arthur thought about the verse in Jeremiah, "Seek the peace and prosperity of the city to which I have carried you into exile. Pray to the Lord for it, because if it prospers, you too will prosper" (Jeremiah 29:7).

After his election to the Yachats City Council, Arthur began to see ways he could work for justice. As he expresses in one of his poems, he set himself the goal of "bringing order out of social clutter." He found that the council meetings had become bogged down in parliamentary maneuvering. Contentious processes got in the way of crafting fair and just solutions for local problems. Drawing on his Quaker commitment to allowing each person to be heard fairly, Arthur helped the council convert its business meetings from the legalistic use of procedural rules to a form of consensus. Routine items were placed on a consent agenda, approved without a vote unless there was objection. The council began discussing major policy issues informally, working together to develop acceptable proposals, assuring that all members had been heard. Even if some members voted against the final proposal, they felt their views had been respected and considered in the discussion.

Arthur also began working for justice by affirming his peers on the council and on the city staff. When he became mayor, an unpaid position, he made the rounds among employees, learning about the work they did and listening to their concerns. When it became necessary for the city to deviate from the normal pay scale to attract a staff person with state-mandated training and certification, Arthur insisted that the salaries of other employees be adjusted appropriately. He was pleased that the negotiation of a new labor contract with city workers went smoothly, for he felt the city workers knew he understood their needs and was doing his best to treat them fairly.

A part of Arthur's challenge as a council member and mayor in a small coastal town was to balance competing interests and find just solutions for conflicting goals. A small group of homeowners outside the city limits historically had access to city water, but the old water pipe along the rocky headlands serving those homes deteriorated. One approach would have been to deny further service to these families. Arthur helped the city staff find a creative and affordable way to repair the system and continue service. He negotiated rates equitable both to them and to the heavily taxed city residents. Justice prevailed without recourse to litigation.

The hospitality industry in Yachats seeks to increase tourism and largely supports the city budget through room taxes. Representing a different point of view, the retirees and other homeowners value the tranquility of a quiet village. Arthur worked to find the mutual interests of these groups, since both groups needed clean water, good roads, effective law enforcement, and an efficient sewer system.

Prior to his career as a professor of philosophy, Arthur had served for a time in the pastoral ministry. As a community leader, he also found opportunities to minister. He spent time with council members when they experienced painful issues in family and personal life. To exercise his ministerial gift as a proclaimer of truth, he decided to write a poem for each meeting of the city council. The poems were then published in the city's newsletter and later gathered into a book. Arthur is probably correct when he speculates that this may be the only city in the country whose meetings regularly began with poems written by the mayor. He could say things as a poet that conveyed in acceptable ways his Christian commitment to principles of justice, fairness, and truth.

The professionals in the community admired his skill with words and some people in the service sector of Yachats looked forward to the next poem from the mayor.

It is fitting to end our glimpse of the work of Arthur Roberts and our look at the concept of justice with this sonnet, written for the Yachats city council:

Sonnet on Local Governance

Governance is not much fun
when people bicker and complain,
when sewers flood from too much rain.
It seems you can't please everyone.
But when all is said and done
troubles wax but also wane.
Civility and truth sustain
eras of good will. For one
whose joy it is to serve another
by making order out of social
clutter, duty to a neighbor
really is a rather special
sort of civic love,
kindled from Above.[21]

CHAPTER EIGHT

Government as an Instrument of Peace

A beautiful prayer, attributed to Francis of Assisi, includes the line, "Lord, make me an instrument of your peace." The prayer echoes the words of Jesus, "Blessed are the peacemakers, for they will be called sons of God" (Matthew 5:9). Other Scriptures, such as James 3:18, lift up the ideal of peacemaking: "Peacemakers who sow in peace raise a harvest of righteousness."

Few would question the idea of working for peace as an abstract goal, but what about the person who is in a position of national leadership when that nation is threatened by huge, menacing armies? Wouldn't most of us in that situation toss aside our peace slogans and take as our motto such Bible verses as Ecclesiastes 3:8, which speaks of a "time for war and a time for peace"?

If anyone had a good reason to abandon peaceful strategies, it was Gideon, leader of the Hebrew nation before there were kings. We call these leaders "judges," but we should not confuse the title with contemporary judges, whose primary function is judicial. Gideon was the national leader, serving like a king without the title. Actually, it was not a good time to become the head of the nation of Israel. Gideon's predecessor, Deborah, one of the few female political leaders in the Bible, had done quite well as the national leader. But the people were not good followers, either of the leaders, or of their real leader, Jehovah God. The story of Gideon

opens with the sad news that the people were constantly choosing
to do evil and were suffering the consequences in the form of harassment from their enemies. These enemies, especially the Midianites, completely outnumbered the Israelites and proceeded to
help themselves to anything of value in the land. The Hebrews
were so intimidated they hid in the mountain caves, terrified that
the Midianites would go from destroying their crops and their
livestock to tracking down and killing the people. *Not a good time
to become the leader of the Hebrews, Gideon!* (See Judges 6.)

Gideon's name meant "tree feller" and "mighty warrior."
But he had not been living up to the courageous meaning of his
name. As a matter of fact, he found a sneaky way to keep the
Midianites from stealing his grain. He threshed it in a winepress,
assuming they would not look there, since it was not grape-
processing time. Hard at work threshing the grain and keeping an
eye out for Midianite crop thieves, Gideon was caught totally off
guard by the greeting of an angel, "The Lord is with you, mighty
warrior." Gideon almost laughed out loud at the angel's message.
He recognized that the angel knew his name meant "mighty warrior." But the deeds of Gideon indicated he had little courage, as
he hid from the enemy, trying to save some of his father's crop.

But Gideon recovered from his amusement about the angel's
greeting and proceeded to question the angel: "If the Lord is with
us, why has all this happened to us? Where are all his wonders
that our fathers told us about when they said, 'Did not the Lord
bring us up out of Egypt?' But now the Lord has abandoned us
and put us into the hand of Midian" (Judges 6:13). Gideon could
have benefited by a bit of coaching on how one talks to God's messengers. And he was wrong about God abandoning the people. It
was the other way around. The people had abandoned God and
were suffering the consequences. But Gideon at least had the courage to express the fear and frustrations of his family and his countrymen. And at least he was willing to take the risk of harvesting
his father's crops instead of hiding in caves.

Senator Mark Hatfield on peacemaking

"It is peace that we all yearn for today. Yet we know that peace is far more than can ever be negotiated at a conference or written into a treaty. It requires not only that hostility be ended but that the needs of people be fulfilled. And peace can never come perfectly among people until peace has come within them. In our day, the call to bring about such peace must be our calling. We who know something of the power and love of Jesus Christ that makes men whole and that yearns to bring together all creation must make it our calling to bring about such peace.

"As long as there is deprivation, suffering, alienation, self-seeking, and exploitation there is no real peace. Peace can come only when needs—physical and spiritual—are fulfilled; for us, peace means far more than simply avoiding conflict. In the Old Testament, the Hebrew word for peace is *shalom*. The full meaning is actually 'wholeness, soundness, completeness.' Peace entails the fulfillment of needs, whether this be within a nation or within an individual. It has both a political and spiritual dimension, and an inner and outer component. A true understanding of peace includes harmony among nations, reconciliation among people, and the well-being of individuals.

"O God, grant us deliverance from the rhetoric of peace when we personally are not willing to do the things which make for peace...to love, to forgive, to use wisely all of your gifts and resources for the good of mankind, and to permit the invasion of the Holy Spirit in the lives of each of us so that peace may be reflected in our homes between husbands and wives, between children and parents, and in commerce between management and labor, between citizens and government, and among all races of men."[22]

Fortunately the angel did not give up on Gideon. The angel said Gideon should at least use the strength he had, which was not much at the time, and go forward as the agent of deliverance for the Hebrews. Gideon was not through asking questions and fortunately for him the angel had not run out of patience. Gideon began asking about a series of things, questions similar to those Moses had expressed when he was called to be the people's leader. When we read the passage, we wonder why it took so long for Gideon to catch on that God was going to empower him for leading the people toward deliverance. But we have to remember how huge the Midianite armies were and how hopeless things looked for the Hebrews at the time.

Many of us have heard the story of the wet and dry fleece. Some may not have noticed this was the last in a succession of God's miracles to assure Gideon of the validity of his call to leadership. The first was pretty spectacular. Gideon prepared an offering of meat and bread. The angel touched the offering with a staff, and it was consumed by fire. Gideon was impressed, enough so that he built an altar. He called the altar, "The Lord is Peace," indicating he was starting to get a glimpse of his coming mission. But the part about solidifying his call to leadership was a bit harder; God instructed him to build another altar. That was the easy part. The hard part was that he was instructed to tear down his father's altar to Baal and to tear down the Asherah pole, also used for worshiping pagan gods. Gideon was becoming more courageous, but he still was not ready to fully trust God. He and his helpers did the altar replacement project in the dark of night, hoping no one would notice. Of course the people noticed and of course they tracked down the culprits. Gideon's father, Joash, himself a worshiper of pagan gods, came to his son's defense and talked the people out of killing Gideon. The miracle in this part of Gideon's story was his deliverance from certain death for desecrating the local holy place. (See Judges 6:17-32.)

As in the case of Moses and the burning bush, God knew Gideon needed some more assurance before going ahead with his mission. So Gideon asked for another sign and proposed that a wool fleece become wet with dew during the night while the ground around it remained dry. God provided the miracle as requested. Taking the chance that he might be stretching God's patience, Gideon then asked for the reverse miracle, a dry fleece on wet ground. God did it, without pointing out the obvious, that Gideon's faith was still pitifully weak

Those who know the "rest of the story" will wonder how Gideon could be presented as an example of a national leader who chose the path of peace over war. But events make it clear that Gideon lived up to his name, mighty warrior, but left it to God to take care of the enemies. Gideon actually became a mighty peacemaker. The seeming contradictions in Gideon's role were there from the beginning of his public leadership. He first did what generals are supposed to do and called all his men to join him for battle. But God had a huge lesson to teach Gideon about the difference between making war and making peace. The response to Gideon's call to arms had been pretty impressive, considering that all the Hebrews knew how terrible their odds were against the Midianites. Thirty-two-thousand warriors showed up to join Gideon's army, expecting a huge battle, expecting that every one of them would be needed, and expecting there could be heavy casualties. To their great surprise, most of them were sent home. The given reason was that there was no room in God's army for those who were afraid. It was amazing there was anyone in the army who was not afraid; 10,000 passed the "shaking in their boots" test. But the point of this reduction in force was not to sort out the cowards from the heroes. The point was for Gideon and the remaining troops to understand that this was going to be God's battle and God's victory. No amount of human courage would rescue them from defeat. As with King Hezekiah in Isaiah's time, there would be only one warrior in this battle and that was Jehovah God (Judges 7:1-3).

On the eve of the big battle, God instructed Gideon to reduce the size of the army even further. When I first heard this story many years ago, I did not understand what difference it made whether soldiers knelt down to drink from the stream or scooped up water to drink from their hands. I think that is exactly the point; it didn't make any difference. God was not looking for exceptionally alert and courageous warriors. He was looking for a handful of men willing to make fools of themselves against a huge army and ready to celebrate God's victory.

God knew Gideon was not going to sleep very well the night before the showdown with the Midianites, so God invited him to go on a spying mission with a particular purpose. It would have been pointless to attempt to verify the size of the armies of Midian. The fact that there were now only three hundred Hebrews against an uncountable number of Midianites did not suggest the need for further military intelligence. But Gideon was not directed to count the enemy soldiers. He was sent to listen to what some of them were saying during the night. They were talking about a dream that sounded like some of those Joseph had interpreted. In the dream a large loaf of bread went rolling into the Midianite camp and destroyed a tent. God provided the interpretation to the Midianite soldier. The dream was an indication of the coming de-feat of the Midianites, not at the hand of Gideon, but through the miraculous power of God. The intended audience for the dream and its interpretation was not the Midianite troops, but Gideon himself, whose remnants of fear and doubt faded away as he hur-ried back to round up the three hundred sleepy Hebrew soldiers.

It was probably good that Gideon did not rehearse the "battle plan" with his troops or he might have ended up with three soldiers instead of three hundred. In place of swords and shields, Gideon gave them trumpets and jars with torches inside. The trumpets were familiar tools to those in the group who knew their Hebrew history, for the blowing of trumpets was part of the events that led to God's miraculous defeat of Jericho under Joshua's leadership. But the jars with torches inside were to be used for a new tactic.

It would be absurd to attribute the battle's victory to Gideon's cleverness and the Midianites' fear as they heard the trumpets and the shouting. Hearing three hundred men shouting in the dead of night would have been startling. But given the size

William Wilberforce on peacemaking

"Yet Christianity does not favor that vehement and inordinate ardor in the pursuit of temporal objects, which progresses toward the acquisition of immense wealth, or of widely spread renown. Real Christianity does not propose to gratify the extravagant views of those mistaken politicians whose chief concern for their country is extended dominion, the command of power, and unrivaled affluence, rather than the most solid advantages of peace, comfort, and security. These men would barter comfort for greatness. In their vain reveries they forget that the nation consists of individuals, and that the true national prosperity is no other than the multiplication of personal happiness.

"Such would be the happy state of a truly Christian nation. This community, peaceful at home, would be respected and beloved abroad. General integrity in all its dealings would inspire universal confidence.

"Differences between nations commonly arise from mutual injuries, and still more from mutual jealousy and distrust. Of the former, there would exist no longer any ground for complaint. The latter would find nothing to attack upon."[23]

of the Midianites' army, Hebrew yelling and trumpet blowing would not have made much of an impression. The point of all this was not surprise and fear; it was a miracle, pure and simple. God stepped in to produce fear when the Midianites had no reason to be afraid. As God had told Gideon and the Hebrews all along, this was not about military cleverness and the power of surprise. This was about God taking matters into his own hands and dealing with the enemy in his own way. This was about some foolish horn blowing and pot smashing by a handful of Hebrews with the courage to obey God and trust that God would deal with the threats to their very existence (Judges 7).

Peacemaking suffers from the misconception that it consists of passivity instead of pacifism. Based on this notion, the peaceful thing for Gideon and the Hebrews to do would have been to sit by and let the Midianites kill them or take them captive. But as is evident from the life of modern peacemakers such as Gandhi and Martin Luther King, Jr., peacemaking is about courage and cleverness. It is a confrontational process, outwitting the enemy, loving the enemy as Jesus taught, taking great risks, but not taking enemy lives. In this sense, Gideon should be the hero of the modern peacemaking movement. Instead we let him remain hidden among the many Old Testament accounts of battles and mislabel him as a warrior instead of a peacemaker.

Many of the Old Testament leaders were actually warriors and they thought obedience to God meant defending their people with military might. But people like Gideon, Jehoshaphat, Joshua, and Hezekiah understood that God was ready to step in and deal directly with the forces of evil. God might call on humans at times to be part of the plan, but he would only do it if these humans would be like the trumpet-blowers and pot-smashers, who knew their efforts meant very little. They were the warm-up act, calling attention to their very weakness and making it clear that the Ruler of the Universe was commander in chief. The call to peace is the call to deal with injustice and oppression, but not in human strength. It is a call to fully trust God.

The psalmist captured the illogical, wonderful truth that the way of peace is the way of trusting God to deliver:

> Now I know that the Lord saves his anointed; he answers him
> from his holy heaven with the saving power of his
> right hand.
> Some trust in chariots and some in horses, but we trust in the
> name of the Lord our God.
> They are brought to their knees and fall, but we rise up and
> stand firm.
> O Lord, save the king!
> Answer us when we call. (Psalm 20:6-9)

What a fitting tribute to Gideon, the foolish trumpet-blower and pot-smasher. Gideon, the man of peace, had the courage to trust God to provide the victory.

MEET LEROY BENHAM

His nickname at one time during his involvement as an active citizen was "The Prophet." That came partly from the bushy beard he has worn most of his adult life. But it was more than that. Those who knew him were aware he was a determined follower of Christ. And though he would not have been inclined to quote the Old Testament prophets in his work on various governing bodies, he stood for the virtues of the prophets—integrity, justice, courage, and peace. He could be a person of few words at times, but when he spoke he offered good solutions to the intense conflicts surrounding him in his political work.

His name is Leroy Benham, retired from owning and managing a small manufacturing business, deeply loyal to his local church, and intensely involved with his large family of children and grandchildren. He was able to juggle his service to all sorts of policy groups with managing a growing business and keeping up his family and church involvements.

Leroy moved from low-key participation in service clubs and business groups into the political milieu when he ran for the local school board. Looking back on the first of his eight years on the board, he might have felt a little like Gideon against the Midianites. In the previous election a group of citizens had campaigned and won election together, promising to rescue the school system from trends they considered excessively liberal. They wanted the schools to get back to basics and considered the teaching of reading with the phonics method to be one of the important ways to return the schools to educational soundness.

Leroy did not object to the use of phonics, but he felt strongly that certain members of the school board were using inappropriate tactics to get their way. They dealt with their opponents harshly and hired a superintendent who reflected their conservative values and their harsh ways of working with teachers, other administrators, and the public. After he was elected and before he took his place on the board, Leroy set about to investigate the background of the incumbent superintendent. Through the information Leroy gathered about this person's previous service, the superintendent lost his credibility and even his supporters turned against him and eventually helped remove him from the position.

For most of the early years on the school board, Leroy had to function with a combination of confrontation and reconciliation. He joined others on the board in confronting an inept administrator and for a time the battle waged furiously. At the same time, he was determined to restore trust, to reconcile people who were at odds with one another, and to restore the centrality of learning instead of civil war. Those who remember that era in the school system in Newberg, Oregon, look back with gratitude that peace was eventually made, trust was restored, and teachers and students were able to get back to their learning goals.

Overlapping with Leroy's service on the school board, he became involved in a county-wide effort to identify unmet needs of the children and youth in the community. Learning of his work in that local effort, the governor appointed Leroy to a new statewide children and youth services committee. He might not have expected this project to turn into another battlefield, but it did. The governor gave this group a mandate different from that of its predecessor and the personnel associated with the previous efforts dug in to defend their turf. The two generals in the mini-battle, attorneys, were adept at doing battle with words. In that battlefield Leroy earned the name "Prophet," for he patiently listened to the struggles of the two factions and found constructive ways out of the impasse. Time after time he drew on his Quaker commitment to peacemaking to help the factions turn from direct combat to dealing with the needs of young people in the state. When he ended his service on the committee four years later, he felt the work of reconciliation had been accomplished. The committee had sponsored initiatives all over the state that addressed the unique situations in each area.

During these active public involvements, he participated in other policy groups, both private and public, also finding in those arenas that his ability to find common ground between opposing factions was an important skill he could offer. Then he took a step toward a more visible political position by filing for election to the state legislature. Those who knew of his contribution to the various public and private policy groups prior to that time felt he was extremely well prepared to serve in the legislature. His campaign was off to a good start. Running unopposed in the Republican primary, he had adequate time to build support prior to the general election in November. But things began to turn against him in the summer between the primary and general elections. His party's county central committee was tightly controlled by a group of individuals who were conservative, as Leroy was and is. They professed to be Christians, as Leroy does. They wanted a strong candidate in the general election, but more than that they wanted Leroy to say exactly the right things on their priority issues.

Looking back on the events that led to Leroy's defeat in the general election, with the benefit of hindsight, he knows what he would do differently. The conservative party leaders were passionate about the principal issue, abortion. Leroy agreed with them that abortion was wrong, but expressed his views in a way that was too moderate for their tastes. His position resembled that of the senior senator from Oregon, who also was pro-life but was also regularly at odds with zealots in the movement who wanted him to support every one of their specific points. Senator Hatfield declined to do that and lost much of their support, but had plenty of other support to continue winning. In his campaign Leroy feels he should have nailed down his position on major issues like abortion very early, rather than puzzling about some of the pro-life details during the campaign. The pro-lifers turned against him and sent out a mailing accusing him of backing away from a firm pro-life position. The opposition of the pro-life group and that of the leaders of Leroy's own party probably cost him the victory in the election.

Leroy's skills as a reconciler and his ability to see the merits in a variety of positions on an issue did not serve him well in his campaign for the legislature. His opponents were willing to give the election to the other party's candidate because Leroy would not agree with them on every point. He served out his term on the school board and has not since been as active in local and statewide issues. But he continues to be an active citizen in other ways and continues with his strong commitment to his family and his church. The state of Oregon lost an opportunity to benefit from the skills of a very strong leader; Leroy was spared some of the headaches that go with participation in public positions. But he has no regrets about the time and energy he has given to active citizenship and especially to peacemaking in the public arena.

CHAPTER NINE

Confronting Government Leaders

He was not the kind of person who spent time in the king's palace. Like John the Baptist in New Testament times, he wore rough-looking clothes made of camel's hair. Elijah, a social misfit, was more comfortable being fed by ravens than dining in the royal household. He did, however, have a standing invitation to visit King Ahab and Queen Jezebel, rulers of the kingdom of Israel, with its capital in Samaria. Actually, though, it was not a social invitation; it was more like being at the top of the "Ten Most Wanted" list of Israel.

King Ahab had good reason to be upset with Elijah. Like those who preceded him and those who followed, Ahab, seventh among 19 kings of Israel, was ungodly, oppressive, and lacking in compassion. He seemed determined to outdo his father, Omri, in the amount of evil he could bring upon the people. Twice in quick succession accounts of Ahab say he did more evil and did more to make God angry than all the preceding kings of Israel (1 Kings 16:30-33).

It was not just that Ahab was indifferent about serving the true God and unwilling to live a righteous life. He went out of his way to turn the people away from God. His wife Jezebel became his chief ally in this process. The very selection of her as queen in-sulted God, for Jezebel was passionate in her service of Baal and other pagan gods. Jezebel was determined to lead the people of Israel in that direction.

We don't know anything about Elijah's early ministry except that he was from a place called Tishbe, and we're not even sure where that was. But Elijah's prophetic ministry was well known and completely unappreciated by King Ahab. Ahab later called Elijah the "troubler of Israel," presumably because Elijah challenged the pagan ways of the national leadership and the values that had corrupted the entire nation.

Elijah's first message to Ahab fit right in with Elijah's reputation as the troublemaker of Israel. He announced that a multi-year drought was about to begin. Considering the terrible experiences of the Hebrew people with droughts, extending back to the famine that forced them to relocate into Egypt, Elijah's message was not good news. After saying something like that, a prophet needs to have a quick escape route in mind. We are not given Ahab's reaction, but if we were writing it today, we would probably have to delete the profanity. We don't know if Jezebel was nearby to hear the prophecy, but we can imagine that her anger would have been even greater than Ahab's. She had convinced the people to put their trust in Baal and Asherah and she probably sensed that these gods had no power to reverse the cycles of nature.

In any event, Elijah did not hang around the palace to see whether he would become the target of the royal anger. Instead, he quickly found a hiding place outside Israel's jurisdiction. After the king's anger had subsided, God sent Elijah to Zarephath, a place north of Israel in what is now Lebanon. This time his provider was not a raven but a widow who had no food and no money. The miraculous way God provided for Elijah's needs through a poor widow helped him understand the certainty of God's provision and the invincibility of God's power. It turned out he needed these lessons a great deal in the days to come. And he needed the kind of affirmation he received from the widow after God brought her son back to life: "Now I know that you are a man of God and that the word of the Lord from your mouth is the truth" (1 Kings 17).

Senator Mark Hatfield on courageous confrontation

"Our faith calls us to seek God's will for man and for the world. We must look at our own country, examine the values that are guiding our culture, and ask whether they are true to God's will and purpose. If not, they must be challenged with a prophetic word, and Christians must witness to the need for national repentance—that is, the need to turn from present ways 'unto the ways of the Lord.'"[24]

God had sent Elijah to tell Ahab there would be a famine. After leaving the widow's house, Elijah went again to Ahab, this time to tell him the famine would end soon. But given the hatred Ahab and Jezebel felt toward Elijah, going back to speak with Ahab was not a safe thing to do. In fact, Obadiah, the king's steward (not Obadiah the prophet), reacted in desperate fear when Elijah asked him to announce his presence to the king. Obadiah had remained faithful to God and had protected a number of the remaining godly prophets. But Obadiah knew the political realities in Samaria. Not only would Elijah's life be at risk if he showed up at the palace, but Obadiah, the messenger, might lose his life as well.

Elijah was a typically courageous prophet but a terrible politician. In spite of the risks involved in going to meet Ahab, he did not in any way water down his message. Ahab had called Elijah a troublemaker and Elijah threw the charge right back at him, saying it was Ahab who had caused all the national difficulties by turning Israel's people away from Jehovah to the worship of Baal. The argument could have gone on a long time, but Elijah knew he could not win this one with words. It would take a dramatic demonstration of God's power, much more than food-bearing ravens and a widow's son brought back to life.

This showdown between Jehovah and Baal was clearly not something Elijah had dreamed up. God had sent him to help the people see the need to turn away from the pagan gods and turn back to Jehovah God. The plan was simple. The four hundred fifty prophets of Baal were to prepare a bull for sacrifice and were allowed to use all of their power and magic to persuade their gods to consume the offering with fire. If they did not succeed, Elijah was to pray to God that the offerings be consumed. The odds were terrible, humanly speaking—four hundred fifty prophets and one bull versus one prophet and one bull. Where did Elijah get this crazy idea? At least that's what Obadiah might have been muttering in the background.

But Ahab liked the plan and it distracted him from his compulsion about killing Elijah. And the people liked the plan. A few of them might have sensed that Jehovah and Elijah would win, even though the odds against them were discouraging. Others were ready to celebrate the humiliation and defeat of this miserable outcast of a prophet who dared challenge the choice of Israel to put their national trust in Baal, the favored god of the region.

While the prophets of Baal were hard at work calling on Baal to bring fire to consume the bull, Elijah calmly watched from a shady place. He could not resist some pointed sarcasm when he checked on their progress after they had spent hours pleading with Baal to send fire. "Perhaps he [Baal] is deep in thought, or busy, or traveling. Maybe he is sleeping and must be awakened," Elijah said. That would have been another good time to have a fast horse nearby. But for some reason the false prophets did not turn their frustrations on Elijah. They prayed more strenuously and tried to impress their gods by cutting their bodies. If sacrificing an animal wouldn't work, maybe they could sacrifice themselves. By then they probably sensed they had little to lose, since their lives were at risk if they did not somehow get the animal to start burning (1 Kings 18:20-29).

The end of the first round of the contest was a sad time for the Baal prophets. As the passage says, "There was no response, no one answered, no one paid attention." What an epitaph for these dead gods! Elijah came from his observation post and began

William Wilberforce on Idolatry

"Scripture sees idolatry, then, as the crime against which God expresses His highest resentment and announces His severest punishment. But let us not deceive ourselves. Idolatry does not consist so much in bowing the knee to idols as it does in expressing internal homage of the heart to them. It consists in feeling toward idols any of that supreme love, or reverence, or gratitude, which God reserved for Himself as His exclusive privilege.

"On the same principle, whatever else draws off the heart from Him, monopolizes our prime attention, and holds the chief place in our respect and affections—that is as much an idol to us as is an image of wood and stone before which we should fall down and worship. The Bible commands the servant of God not to set up his idol in his heart. It therefore repeatedly terms sensuality and covetousness *idolatry*."[25]

preparing for round two of the contest. Again, he had no fast horse and no escape route in sight. And again, Obadiah might have been watching and wondering why Elijah was making the contest even more difficult by asking that large quantities of water be brought to douse the wood and the pieces of meat. One drenching was not enough to set up a clear demonstration of God's power. At Elijah's direction, water was poured on the altar three times. *Not too smart, Elijah!*

The prayers to Baal had been long, eloquent, and passionate. Elijah's prayer to God was elegantly simple:

"O Lord, God of Abraham, Isaac and Israel, let it be known today that you are God in Israel and that I am your servant and have done all these things at your command. Answer me, O Lord, answer me, so these people will know that you, O Lord, are God, and that you are turning their hearts back again." (1 Kings 18:36-37)

The outcome of the "extreme games" of Samaria contained high drama. God's fire not only consumed the bull and the wood, but the stones and dirt as well. There was also gruesome bloodshed; the Baal prophets did not live to talk about their defeat. Finally, there was athletic heroism; Elijah outran Ahab's chariots, covering the 17 miles to Ahab's summer palace before the king's fastest horses could get there. The drama of Elijah's post-victory experiences is well worth reading in the book of 1 Kings, for a time of wrenching fear and deep depression followed his triumph. Fortunately, God delivered him from the depression and called on him to deliver yet another unpopular message to yet another ungodly king of Israel, Ahaziah. This time the fire from God consumed the king's messengers. Then Elijah appeared before the king to tell him he would die. The king did indeed die, but Elijah bypassed physical death, getting a ride in an amazing chariot of fire bound for heaven (2 Kings 1 — 2).

One can get lost in the exciting events of Elijah's life and miss the heart of the message — there is one true God and no pseudo-god can match his power, his justice, and his goodness. But the important subtext of the passage relates directly to the theme of this book:

> **Some people are called to risk personal harm and disfavor to deliver unpopular messages to their national leaders. Elijah showed extraordinary courage and eloquence in delivering his message to the king. Citizens today may not face such dramatic opportunities to deliver their messages of truth, but dare not be any less courageous.**

One of the many tragedies of President Richard Nixon's presidential career was the willingness of his closest advisors to engage in criminal behavior to assure his reelection. Charles Colson, who has since become an influential Christian leader, wishes today that he and his coworkers had been as courageous as Elijah in confronting the wrongdoing of their boss, the president.

There are at least three types of courageous confrontation to which Christian citizens may be called:

✓ **Staff members of public officials** — Like Charles Colson, people serve as staff members at the federal, state, county, and local level. They are selected for their competence, their interest in public service, their moral courage, and their loyalty. The problem arises if they have lots of loyalty but not enough moral courage. They may be unwilling to risk their political career by challenging the actions of the public official for whom they work. This is a problem, since staff members are generally not protected by civil service laws and can thus be fired without recourse. But Elijah's courage should guide their conduct.

✓ **People with access to public officials** — The prophet Nathan provides an excellent example of an individual who was a friend of King David. When David made an idiot of himself by committing adultery with Bathsheba and arranging for the death of her husband, Nathan had the courage to go to David and name his evil behavior. This timely rebuke was the first step in David's restoration into right relationship with God.

✓ **Individual citizens as confronters** — Apathy is the enemy of effectively influencing government. The idea that one person cannot impact national evils is a form of apathy. Most national reforms can be traced to the courage of a few who could not tolerate the status quo. William Wilberforce had considerable help in combating slavery in England, but his personal initiative and his amazing persistence were essential to the outcome of the struggle. Likewise, individual citizens can begin the process of challenging local, state, and national leaders. Individual voices can be amplified in the media and by supportive citizen groups. Accountability can begin with one person seeing a discrepancy between a public official's conduct and God's standards.

MEET KEVIN SNARR

Kevin is a veteran of a decade of service on the city council in Wilmington, Ohio. But you would not know he has that much experience in politics from his youthful appearance. Kevin got involved in politics right out of college. His "day job" has been in public education, first as a classroom teacher and now in his second position as a principal. Like many small towns, Wilmington has no city manager, so council members have to participate in supervision and management, as well as policy making. Being on city council is a big job with almost no pay. A little public recognition serves as a reward, but the council members are only a phone call away from hostile citizens.

Reflecting on ten years in city government, Kevin feels his most significant efforts have been in exercising responsible stewardship over the land. Ohio, like many states, has few restrictions on expanding city boundaries into farmland. It falls to local officials like Kevin to deal with the problem of small-scale urban sprawl. Land outside the city boundaries is relatively cheap, so developers purchase farmland, then ask that their plans for residential and commercial development be approved. They then seek to have their property annexed so they can get water lines, sewer service, streets, and public safety services.

Recently Kevin has felt like David facing Goliath, questioning the relocation and expansion plans of two huge retail chains. In both cases the Goliaths won, but Kevin has kept working to protect locally owned businesses. He wants to put the priority on developing land inside the city rather than using the open land outside city boundaries. At the same time he has worked to preserve open space in the city for parks and scenic preservation. In these struggles he has had to decide whether to take on political battles he might not win and whether his actions will jeopardize the political support he needs for future endeavors.

CHAPTER TEN

God and the Public
Are Watching

The cases were painfully similar, but their outcomes very different. Two heads of state embarrassed themselves, their families, and their constituents with their personal behavior. Both of them were unable to stifle their lustful thoughts about the attractive young women who surrounded them. Both of them went beyond lustful thinking to lustful behavior and brought tragedy to their own lives and especially to the women to whom they were attracted. Both of them could have justified their conduct by pointing to similar behavior by other heads of state in their own time and historically. Both of them could have rationalized their behavior as a harmless way to cope with the pressures of their responsibilities. Both of them somehow thought their conduct would escape the notice of the average citizen and that they could continue to maintain public trust while engaging in inappropriate sexual behavior.

The differences between the two cases, King David and Bill Clinton, are substantial. A godly prophet confronted David with his actions and David was profoundly repentant. Undoubtedly godly people confronted President Clinton about his wrong actions, but the public saw little indication of the remorse and repentance that David felt and expressed. Clinton was also able to keep his office, but not because he acknowledged that his actions were wrong and repented of the harm he brought to his sexual partners and his family. He used his legal skills to outmaneuver his foes in the impeachment process and finished his term as president with remarkably few scars from his behavior.

David should have known better. God had selected him from among all the young men of Israel for his humble and godly spirit. In David's first experience in national politics he served as understudy to a king who was equally gifted and equally godly in his early years. But King Saul forgot that his power came from God and began to cross the line into the spiritual leadership functions he as political leader was not allowed to exercise. Saul's self-confidence turned to arrogance and descended to paranoia, as he began to imagine that the young David was a threat to his reign and must be eliminated. David should have learned from Saul that misusing power results in terrible consequences.

It would have been wonderful if David's experience with lustful behavior had mirrored the conduct of Joseph, who also had an encounter with lust. To his credit, Joseph let his conscience control his hormones and rejected the attempted seduction of his boss's wife. He literally ran away, clutching the clothes his temptress had not already removed from him and went on to live a life of godly courage and moral strength. David, by contrast, earned an F in dealing with lust. It was springtime and David had extra time on his hands and an eye for attractive ladies. His competent general, Joab, was successfully leading the troops in battle against the nation's enemies. There was little for David to do but wait for reports of each day's battles and to pace around on the roof of the palace. Unfortunately the palace was taller than the buildings around it; this gave David a clear view of the neighbors on their private rooftops.

In most cases when David walked on the palace roof there was nothing to see, just clothes hanging out to dry in the evening breeze. Sometimes one could see a few men sipping wine and discussing the day's business transactions or clusters of women talking about their families, hoping the children were all asleep. Nothing was worth noticing as the evening shadows lengthened.

William Wilberforce on sexual temptation

"Some take up with sensual pleasures. The chief happiness of their lives consists in one species or another of animal gratification. Remember, it is not our purpose to speak of the gross and scandalous profligates who renounce all claims to the name of Christ. But we speak of those who maintain a certain decency of character and who perhaps tolerably observe the forms of religion—those we describe as sober sensualists. Though less impetuous and more regulated in their lifestyle, they are not less staunch and steady in pursuit of their favorite objects than the professed devotees of licentious pleasures."[26]

But wait! What is that in the courtyard just to the north of the palace? It's an incredibly beautiful woman finishing her bath, oblivious to the possibility of being seen by someone on the palace roof—such a gorgeous woman!

Take a cold shower, David! You're happily married; she's probably married as well. Nothing will be gained by turning your sexual fantasies into sexual behavior. But it won't hurt to find out who she is and what her circumstances are, rationalized King David. One of his staff was able to identify her, to put a name with the great body. And sure enough, this was a married woman, off limits to David, even if he chose to invoke the royal privilege of having multiple wives. There would have been absolutely no way David could have prayed to God about his desires and received the green light to pursue his interest in this woman. Of course he didn't pray about it. Without giving time for his passions to cool down, he sent his staff to bring Bathsheba to him while he waited in the royal bedchamber.

If the biblical account had been written like a modern novel, it would have included minute details of David and Bathsheba's night of passion. Fortunately, we're spared that in 2 Samuel. David was attractive, warm-hearted, and provided affection to a woman whose husband was away in battle. Whatever misgivings Bathsheba might have had about being unfaithful to her husband would have been overcome by the fact that this was her husband's commander in chief. They had a pleasant night together, not a problem for the moral codes of many people at that time, or today.

And then there was the morning after. Not the morning-after pill. That didn't exist then. The morning after when Bathsheba realized she might become pregnant and it would be obvious to her husband Uriah that this was not his child. He had been away in combat. Bathsheba was worried, but David was way ahead of her. David called Uriah to the palace, was gracious to him, and encouraged him to spend the night with his wife. Unfortunately for David, Uriah felt he shouldn't spend the night in the comforts of his home while his fellow soldiers were camped in the hills around Rabbah. In spite of all David's efforts, including getting Uriah drunk, Uriah stayed among the servants in the palace rather than enjoying the pleasure of being home with his wife.

David was stuck. Uriah had not cooperated with the plot to hide the results of David's night with Bathsheba. David's fear and guilt turned to anger and during the night he determined he would try to hide his adultery by committing murder. Not murder with his own hands; not killing Uriah himself, like he had done with Goliath. But murder in the form of a note to General Joab giving instructions that Joab was to arrange for Uriah's death on the front lines. It was not a problem for Joab to arrange for the death of yet another soldier. He had heard a rumor about David spending some time with Uriah's wife, so he knew the purpose of the king's note. He also figured out that arranging for Uriah's death would distract the king from being upset that the battle was not going well. Little progress was being made in the siege of the fortified city of Rabbah. Joab knew the king would not complain as long as the battle report contained news of the regrettable death of a number of soldiers, including the husband of Bathsheba (2 Samuel 11).

The hero of this part of David's story was a prophet with whom David had already interacted regarding the plan to build a temple for God. Nathan had first been very positive about the idea of building a temple. He thought it logical to build a beautiful place of worship to symbolize the place of God at the center of the kingdom. But Nathan got the message from God that it was not the time to build the temple, that David's son Solomon was to have that privilege and responsibility. If David was disappointed when Nathan gave him this word, it wasn't apparent from his long and beautiful prayer recorded in 2 Samuel 7. The prayer ended with this moving benediction:

> "Now be pleased to bless the house of your servant, that it may continue forever in your sight; for you, O Sovereign Lord, have spoken, and with your blessing the house of your servant will be blessed forever." (2 Samuel 7:29)

David had it right; the point was not in building an impressive temple. The whole point of the Covenant was to continue in absolute faithfulness to God, keeping God at the center of the kingdom. David got the part about the temple, but didn't fully "get it" when it came to absolute faithfulness. He spent a miserable few months awaiting the birth of Bathsheba's son, enjoying her company, but he was unable to escape the guilt of his actions. He put words to those guilty feelings in one of his songs:

> When I kept silent, my bones wasted away through my groaning all day long.
> For day and night your hand was heavy upon me;
> my strength was sapped as in the heat of summer.
> (Psalm 32:3-4)

God and Nathan let David suffer with his guilt for most of a year. Bathsheba gave birth to a healthy child. Uriah was forgotten as just another casualty of war. The royal staff members were discreet enough to abstain from gossiping about the circumstances of David's acquisition of a new wife. Enter Nathan, trusted prophet of God, in a long line of prophets who brought unwelcome messages to kings and subjects. Nathan, the gifted storyteller. Nathan, the prophet willing to risk his life to deliver the lines, "You are the man!"

David had a special nostalgia about sheep, even though he had no intention of going back to being a shepherd. But lambs were always cute and always helpless. When Nathan told about a man who was so poor he owned only one sheep and this sheep had literally become a part of the family, David understood. He had grown very fond of his family's sheep as a boy. They were cuddly creatures, in need of someone strong to protect them. But Nathan's story took a surprising twist. The rich man in town seized the lamb to become the main course for dinner with an out-of-town guest, leaving the poor man without his pet lamb.

"What an outrageous thing to do!" exploded David. "The man had hundreds of sheep and cattle he could have used for the evening barbecue. I won't stand for such cruel and oppressive behavior. Bring him to me and I'll have him put to death!"

"Well, David, I can't very well bring the guilty party to you," said Nathan. "You see, this is a story that illustrates some tragic events in your own life. You're the rich man, possessing all you could ever want. Many women in the kingdom would have been honored to be your wife. You had an unlimited choice. But you had to take the cherished companion of a poor man, one of your soldiers out in battle. You stole the little lamb. Not only have you brought great harm to one family, but more importantly, you have defied the God who assured you of his unlimited blessing if you would only obey him without fail." (See 2 Samuel 12:1-10.)

There was good news and bad news after David got the point of the story. He could not deny the wrongness of what he had done. He did the one thing he could do. He repented and pled with God for mercy. He recorded that confession in a psalm:

> Then I acknowledged my sin to you and did not cover up my
>   iniquity.
> I said, "I will confess my transgressions to the Lord" — and you
>   forgave the guilt of my sin. (Psalm 32:5)

Nothing to it, right? You get caught in sinful behavior and you turn to a merciful God who is always willing to forgive the repentant sinner. Well, yes, but it is important to be clear about the outcome of David's pleading to God for mercy. Nathan not only exposed his king's wrongdoing, but also told him there would be two unpleasant consequences. Some of his wives would be unfaithful to him in the future. That didn't worry David too much; the problem was the second consequence. The son born to Bathsheba would die. God would completely forgive and restore David, but would not heal the child's sickness. No amount of agonizing prayer would change the final chapter in the story of David's sin. He and Bathsheba would have other children, one of them his successor to the throne, but David would always ache because of the stupidity of his adulterous and murderous actions. Thanks to the grace of God and David's repentance, he was marvelously restored to fellowship with God and to his place as spiritual leader of his nation. In the words of one of the psalms about repentance:

> Blessed is he whose transgressions are forgiven, whose sins are
> covered.
> Blessed is the man whose sin the Lord does not count against
> him
> and in whose spirit is no deceit.
> Many are the woes of the wicked, but the Lord's unfailing love
> surrounds
> the man who trusts in him. (Psalm 32:1-2, 10)

A profound contradiction exists in the expectations of the American public regarding the behavior of their governmental leaders. We often feel outrage and contempt toward a person who behaves immorally or illegally. But the public disdain for wrong behavior often stops short of holding public officials accountable for their wrong behavior. In general, we aren't willing to say with Nathan, "You are the one!" Clinton, though impeached, was not convicted. The senators who had his fate in their hands were conscious of the public sentiment that a leader's personal life should not disqualify him from continuing as a leader. Time after time voters have reelected officials found guilty of personal and public wrongdoing. Time after time the public has condemned their conduct but allowed them to stay in office. Why? Because the average person wants to avoid the consequences of his or her own wrongdoing if caught. They want to be able to escape by saying their personal life is no one else's business. When that person is a minister or evangelist, those excuses rarely work. But most people argue there were no victims of their adultery and deceit, even though their actions have inflicted deep emotional scars on their spouses and children.

In the public arena people expect public officials to lead exemplary lives but are surprisingly tolerant toward those who betray the public trust through their wrong actions. What is lacking is adherence to a basic principle that guides the follower of Christ:

God has a high standard of right behavior for those who are given positions of leadership. They are expected to live as if God and the public were watching every one of their actions and were listening to every one of their conversations.

The moral standard for public leaders is actually identical to the standard for every serious follower of Christ. However, the consequences of betraying the public trust are greater for the leader. This standard is captured in the word *integrity*, which in its Latin roots means wholeness and completeness, and by extension, complete honesty and trustworthiness. Absence of integrity caused Jesus to condemn the Pharisees and compare them with whitewashed tombs, attractive on the outside but filled with dead bodies.

People lacking in integrity have mastered the skills of deception, drawing on their talent for impressing people with words about public trust and national uprightness. They speak out against abortion while fathering illegitimate children. They condemn drunken driving while drinking excessively in private. They use their political platform to bemoan the nation's moral decay and pretend they are pure within. They fit the description the

Mark Hatfield on Integrity

"The solution to the problem of immorality in public office begins with the character of the people of this nation. It must begin with us as we search our hearts and consciences. Ask yourself these questions: 'If everyone else in America were just like me, what kind of country would this be? If everyone took the same interest in government that I do, what kind of government would we have? If everyone obeyed the law, including traffic laws, with the same faithfulness that I do, what kind of crime rate would we have? If everyone accepted public service or community work with the same attitude that I do, how much would get done for the public good? If everyone obeyed his conscience and the spiritual commandments of God with the same faithfulness and courage that I do, what kind of world would this be?'

"We should remember that the Congress, the executive branch—indeed, government at all levels—are no better than the demands of the citizens. If the people pursue excellence, they can require it from their public officials. If the nation seeks after righteousness, then its leaders should surely point the way. If each of us, as citizens, expects moral and ethical leadership in government, we ought to be prepared to render that kind of service ourselves whenever called on to do so. By the quality of our own ethical and spiritual character we ought to be setting the standards for conduct, both private and public."[27]

apostle Paul gave of those guilty of sin:

> They have become filled with every kind of wickedness, evil, greed and depravity. They are full of envy, murder, strife, deceit and malice. They are gossips, slanderers, God-haters, insolent, arrogant and boastful; they invent ways of doing evil; they disobey their parents; they are senseless, faithless, heartless, ruthless. Although they know God's righteous decree that those who do such things deserve death, they not only continue to do these very things but also approve of those who practice them. (Romans 1:29-32)

The last phrase of the passage is the punch line in Paul's condemnation of respectable people who practice evil. Paul says it is bad enough that people keep doing these things, but worse that they give approval to others who they know are acting in these ways. In the political context, this is a direct judgment against the false notion that a leader's personal conduct should be of no concern to the citizen. While we cannot expect every citizen, follower of Christ or not, to get the point of this, Christians should at least be consistent about their expectation and God's expectation that leaders be people of integrity.

We cannot join in the widespread tolerance of sinful and immoral behavior on the grounds that the person is doing many good things and we would not want to hinder that good work. We can hope that the expectation of Christians that their political leaders be people of integrity will rub off on those who are not people of Christian faith. High moral expectations of leaders can be shaped by Christian standards and held by Christians and non-Christians alike.

It was my privilege to serve on the staff of Senator Mark Hatfield for a number of years and I have since been able to team-teach with him at George Fox University. It is gratifying to be able to say that in almost thirty years of contact with him, I have not known of any lack of personal and spiritual integrity. For every Bill Clinton, there are other officials like Mark Hatfield, people of integrity who conduct themselves as though God and every one of their constituents were listening to every conversation and watching every action. We should not descend into cynicism and conclude that integrity is not possible, that we should never expect completely moral behavior from our political leaders.

The apostle Paul quotes from Psalms to express a negative view of human integrity:

"There is no one righteous, not even one; there is no one who understands, no one who seeks God. All have turned away, they have together become worthless; there is no one who does good, not even one." (Romans 3:10-12)

But Paul challenges the assertion in this passage that no one is capable of right actions. Paul agrees that no one is capable in his or her own power, but through God's power anyone can live a life of integrity:

> Therefore do not let sin reign in your mortal body so that you obey its evil desires. Do not offer the parts of your body to sin, as instruments of wickedness, but rather offer yourselves to God, as those who have been brought from death to life; and offer the parts of your body to him as instruments of righteousness. For sin shall not be your master, because you are not under law, but under grace. (Romans 6:12-14)

If only King David had allowed God to help control his body and to resist the temptation to engage in wicked behavior, he would have been spared some tragedies. But we would have missed out on a great lesson about integrity. There is no way to be consistent with God's expectations of us while tolerating private wrongdoing. And we have no way of acting as a responsible citizen while tolerating wrongdoing among our public leaders. We should extend the same spirit of mercy and forgiveness to them that God extended to David, but we cannot tolerate wrong actions by covering them with cheap grace. The Bible teaches us that mercy is to be balanced by accountability. God forgave David, but God allowed David to suffer the consequences of his wrong actions. We have no right to be more tolerant of wrong action than God. One of our principal callings as godly citizens is to be God's instruments, insisting on integrity among our leaders.

MEET MARK KROEKER

He arrived at his second point in a very effective commencement speech. Giving a commencement speech is not easy; the graduates want to get the speech out of the way so they can get their diplomas and receive the congratulations of their friends. But this speaker knew how to mix in a little humor, to share his life experiences, to speak forcefully, and above all, to keep it short. He got an A+ in commencement speaking. His second point in the talk was about the power of personal integrity. He linked it with his remarks about the power of persevering tenacity and the power of perfect love. He did a great job of getting some important points across to the graduates at George Fox University.

The speaker, Mark Kroeker, had traveled an unusual life journey to become the chief of police in a major city. His early years were spent among Mennonites in Dallas, Oregon. He has vivid memories of another portion of his growing-up years as part of a missionary family in Congo. He testifies emphatically about his salvation experience as a teenager and his determination to serve Christ during his law enforcement career. His is not a Barney Fife kind of police career, serving small towns where petty theft is the only crime. He served 32 years in the Los Angeles police department, going from sergeant to deputy chief, serving in that city during major riots. As chief in Portland, Oregon, he dealt with all sorts of difficult issues in his years in that position. He has also assisted with police reform efforts in places of intense violence and injustice such as Rwanda and Haiti.

Chief Kroeker challenged the graduates of George Fox to maintain their personal integrity in an environment in which there are few moral absolutes. He called on them to stand firmly when they might otherwise be pulled away from the standards found in the Word of God. Kroeker testified that he had no moral strength apart from the strength he received directly from God. He quoted Philippians 4:13, "I can do everything through him who gives me strength." He said anything good he had been able to accomplish in his life was directly the result of God working in him.[28]

CHAPTER ELEVEN

Other-Service, Not Self-Service

They just didn't get it. Time after time Jesus had talked with his disciples about servanthood and had demonstrated what he meant. Time after time the disciples made it clear they were stuck in worldly ways of dominance, not servanthood. But Jesus kept teaching about it and kept demonstrating it, right up until his last hours with the disciples.

Jesus had a troubling way of being able to hear all the things the disciples were saying on their walks from one place of ministry to another. This time they thought he had not heard their argument. They thought he was busily talking with other disciples in the front of the procession and that the ones in back were out of earshot. What an embarrassment when they got to their destination to have him ask what they had been arguing about. He knew, of course. They didn't want to answer his question, but they didn't need to. They knew they were about to get one of his mini-sermons and they knew they had it coming.

"If anyone wants to be first, he must be the very last, and the servant of all," Jesus said, after the disciples had gathered around. They all looked at each other innocently, but a few of them could not hide their guilt for having tried to figure out a way to become the "first among equals." It was a short sermon. To drive home the point, he found a child nearby, invited him into the circle, and gave him a big hug. He then said to the disciples that if they really understood what Jesus had been teaching, they would spend their time looking for people who needed their love and service. They would seek people who had no power or prestige, just like the child, people who had no way to return their favors and attention (Mark 9:33-37).

It would be nice if we could say the disciples learned the lesson about servanthood after hearing Jesus' teaching and his demonstration about showing love to a child. Unfortunately, that was not the case. One of the most embarrassing evidences that they did not "get it" was a favor two of the "inner circle" of disciples, James and John, asked at a later time. In their minds it was probably not a big deal. They were not asking for anything immediately. They were looking ahead to when they would be with him in heaven. At least they had figured out that their master was God, not just another teacher. It seemed only fair to ask that they be able to sit at his immediate right and left in the heavenly kingdom. In the Gospel of Matthew we are told it was actually the mother of James and John who brought up the subject (Matthew 20:20-21). Maybe the three of them had cornered Jesus and the sons didn't have the nerve to ask about it at first.

James and John deserved an angry response from Jesus. What right did they have, really, to ask for a special place in heaven? Did they deserve to be closer to Jesus than Abraham, Moses, David, and all the other great people of the Old Testament? Did they even have a right to a place of preference over the other disciples? What a disgusting thing for them to ask! Jesus let them off with a fairly mild rebuke. He cautioned them that they probably would not do very well in enduring the suffering he would face and thus would not be entitled to a special place in God's kingdom. A loose translation of his response might be, "I'm so sorry that you're clueless enough to ask for such a thing. I hope you catch on eventually."

Jesus then made a fascinating leap from their inappropriate question into the world of politics to find an example of the difference between dominating and serving. He called the other ten disciples together to hear his lesson on this subject. When the ten realized why he was returning to the topic of humility and servanthood, they pretended to be above the antics of James and John. But Jesus knew that none of them had grasped his teachings about servanthood. He asked them to think about the principal characteristic of human relationships in politics and government. Obviously, it was power.

The name of the game was gaining power and exercising it in whatever way one could. They knew that. The "rulers of the Gentiles" he mentioned were the Roman rulers who governed Palestine. Everything they did reflected the realities of the power they exercised over their subjects in Palestine. It must have hurt for the disciples to have their behavior compared with the power politics of the Romans. But they had it coming. They thought of their master as a great teacher and leader and assumed that their special place at his side entitled them to special privileges. Not so, said Jesus. He had come to demonstrate a different kind of power, based on serving others. They must throw out their ideas of power and start watching what he did, to constantly look for those with needs and to minister to those needs. Maneuvering for special favors was not only wrong, it was a complete contradiction to their work as his followers.

When we notice a repeated theme in Jesus' life and teaching, we can conclude two things about it. First, it must have been very important. Second, it must not have sunk in the first time. Both were true of Jesus' teaching about servanthood. Closer to the end of his life and ministry Jesus sensed that he needed to return to the issue of servanthood. This time another member of the inner circle of disciples had to squirm when it became apparent he did not understand what Jesus was saying. In the amazing foot-washing episode, Jesus gave a whole sermon through a few simple actions. The text doesn't say he realized he needed to come back to the servanthood issue and needed a demonstration to get the point across to the disciples. But that's apparent from the context. James and

John had made fools of themselves for asking for the most privileged positions in heaven. Peter also made himself look ridiculous when Jesus began washing the disciples' feet, questioning whether it was right for his master to serve him in an act of complete humility. He had no idea that servanthood meant receiving acts of kindness as well as humbly serving others.

Peter appeared almost comical at times. Jesus told him he had only two choices—submit to the foot washing or completely drop out of the role of a special follower of Jesus. "Not a problem, Jesus, you can wash my feet, my hands, and even my head," Peter responded. Fortunately Jesus was extraordinarily patient with his disciples. Most of us would have dumped the wash basin on Peter for his sarcastic response. Peter got a C- in servanthood, but the experience may have helped him to start getting the point.

The time Jesus spent sharing the Passover meal with the disciples was an amazing time of tender affection, with some vivid warnings of what was ahead for all of them. It was a time to assure the disciples of Jesus' unlimited love for them and a time to reveal that one of them would not have the courage to claim him as master. And one wouldn't have the good sense to choose loyalty to his master over a chance to earn a few pieces of silver. Three of the gospel accounts have the story of the "Last Supper," but only Luke's story reports on two arguments that reflect the huge gaps in the disciples' understanding. They first argued over whether it was possible for one of them to betray him and if it was, who that might be.

The other argument went back to their lingering desire for power and privilege. Put yourself in Jesus' position. He had just shared bread and wine with them as a way of showing his special love for them, evident throughout his ministry and soon to be even more apparent in his coming death. This moment has found its way in one form or another into one of the most sacred of Christian worship experiences. Did the disciples sit there reverently, reflecting on what Jesus might have meant about the wine and bread symbolizing the giving of his life for them? No, Jesus barely had the cup and plate of bread set down when the disciples

Senator Mark Hatfield on servanthood

"The man committed to Christ is a servant, though he may also be a leader. Following the example of Jesus, he serves for the sake of service, not for the rewards it may bring his way. He cannot isolate himself from the needs of the world, and when he encounters those needs, he is compelled to try to fill them. For him, complacency is not a live option. He knows he should be no less concerned for man's total well-being than was Christ, who instructed that 'whoever would be great among you must be your servant, and whoever would be first among you must be slave of all' (Mark 10:43-44, RSV).

"Another intensified problem for the public servant is that it is easy to forget what it means to serve. True service permits neither condescension nor exploitation. The imagery of the 'public servant' is a fundamental part of the Judeo-Christian tradition. From the servant image of Isaiah to the commands of Christ, we are called to serve others—'the public.' Our call to service is not because service has been earned, but rather because each man is of divine worth. Christ provides the example for the Christian in public service. 'If I then, your Lord and Teacher, have washed your feet, you also ought to wash one another's feet' (John 13:14, RSV). One's spiritual life should help to renew daily a personal sense of 'servanthood.'"[29]

returned to their ongoing struggle for a place of power. When they should have been overwhelmed with wonder at being eyewitnesses to the greatest events of human history, they began arguing about who would be the greatest. *What a disgusting bunch of disciples!* (See Luke 22:7-23.)

When Jesus had to repeat his teaching about servanthood, almost word for word, the disciples should have felt bad. It was like being told the questions on the final exam and then not bothering to prepare the answers. Jesus went back to the teaching he had given the disciples after James and John had asked for a special place in heaven. The context was Roman politics and the teaching was that they as his followers should not emulate the Roman rulers who made a point of showing their subjects how important and powerful they were. Jesus then added an interesting detail to his earlier description of the Gentile politicians. He said they wanted to be seen as "benefactors" of the people. They wanted to use the resources they had at their disposal to win the favor of the people, to make them beholden to them. They gained power by judiciously dispensing the resources and privileges they had at their disposal, by appearing to be generous for the sake of strengthening their own power positions (Luke 22:24-25).

This comment by Jesus brings us to a central concept of Christian citizenship:

> **To be a Christian citizen is to embody Jesus' example and teaching of servanthood. Conventional wisdom in politics says that you cultivate the favor of those who can help you in return. Your every act of generosity to others is calculated to win support, especially from those who have the means to help you stay in power. Every action is based on mutuality and reciprocity. Every action is meant to stimulate others to give their votes, their loyalty, and their political contributions. You don't waste your time being nice to the powerless, especially to those who don't vote. They have nothing to give in return. Every political action is calculated to motivate an equal or greater reaction. You spend time with the newspaper editors, the mayors, and the party chairpersons. They can return your favors. They can assure that you can stay in power. There is no time in this conventional political ethic for washing feet, unless the cameras are rolling and unless your acts of humility will enhance your image and increase your power.**

Robert Greenleaf combined two common words into one concept and coined the phrase "servant leadership." The phrase has become almost a cliché, but Greenleaf did a great service for us in writing his book *Servant Leadership: A Journey in the Nature of Legitimate Power and Greatness*.[30] He talked about leadership in many settings, including higher education. His ideas are important to our understanding of public citizenship as well. Early in his

William Wilberforce on servanthood

"We learn we should repress and extinguish that spirit of arrogance and self-importance which is so natural to the heart of man. It should be our habitual care to cherish and cultivate the lowly tempers. Because of the natural advantages we have over others, and also because of all our moral superiority, we need to depend entirely on the unmerited goodness of God.

"It is undeniably clear that, in the judgment of the Word of God, the love of worldly admiration and applause is basically corrupt. For it tends to exalt and aggrandize ourselves; to pride ourselves on our natural or acquired endowments; or to assume credit and merit for our own qualities. It chooses this self-esteem instead of ascribing all honor and glory where they are due. It is false, therefore, because it exalts that which we should demean. It is also criminal because it intrudes on the privilege of God.

"Since we should set our affections on heavenly things and converse about heavenly objects—and since we should supremely and habitually desire the love and favor of God—then it follows that the love of human applause must be unhealthy. For it tends to draw down our attention to earthly concern, and to bound our desires within the narrow limits of this world. Since it is impure—colored by the tendency to desire and love too much the good opinions and commendation of man—we should view it with suspicion."[31]

book Greenleaf explained the difference between the person who was primarily interested in leadership and the one who saw service as the central feature of that leadership:

> The difference manifests itself in the care taken by the servant—first to make sure that other people's highest priority needs are being served. The best test, and difficult to administer, is: Do those served grow as persons? Do they, while being served, become healthier, wiser, freer, more autonomous, more likely themselves to become servants? And, what is the effect on the least privileged in society; will they benefit, or, at least,

not be further deprived?[32]

To connect Greenleaf's thoughts with Jesus' foot-washing example, it is important to note that Jesus was not just teaching about humility. He also wanted to make his dear friends feel comfortable at the end of a tiring day. Foot washing felt good for those whose feet were tired and dusty. Washing his disciples' feet met an important physical need they had and Jesus meant for his disciples to understand they were not only to do acts of humility, but also to do things that meet important human needs.

Not long ago I was with a group of students in Haiti, learning about some of the pressing national needs and the ways a particular ministry had addressed those needs. Our accommodations were simple but adequate. Unfortunately, the plumbing system in our guesthouse chose to rebel and twice we came into our rooms to find a small lake. We hoped it was water coming directly from the spring, not water from the toilets. Visitors in Third World settings are treated well and there are usually those nearby whose job it is to make them comfortable. We could have summoned the "house help" to clean up the mess. Instead, we found towels, brooms, and surplus T-shirts to deal with the flood ourselves. We had the right to turn the messy job over to someone else, but fortunately we chose to get ourselves a little dirty and to exercise a bit of servanthood. As we sloshed around in the wastewater, we realized our feet were getting washed, but not exactly the way Jesus did it. We enjoyed laughing at our little lesson in serving instead of being served.

Public officials have a particular challenge to keep their focus on serving others. They are constantly given special honor. I was a junior at George Fox College when Governor Mark Hatfield came for his first visit to be with students. We were impressed, but we had no idea how to act in the presence of the highest elected official in the state. We wondered if we should bow and curtsy, but that didn't seem to fit the times. If we had been in the military, we would have known how to salute such a high-ranking person. So we did our best to show respect. Some years later when he was a U.S. senator, I noticed the same thing. People wanted to treat him like royalty and he did his best to assure them he was an ordinary person, not of royal blood.

At least once a year the faculty and administrators of most colleges and universities put on their caps and gowns to march into commencement to honor those about to receive their degrees. If the truth were known, the faculty members and administrators rather enjoy being seen in their academic regalia. What they wear is much nicer than the gowns of the graduates. And if you look closely, you will see that the caps and gowns are not all equal. The robes of those with doctoral degrees have velvet stripes on the sleeves and fancy hoods. And for those whose degrees are from the finest universities in the world, special colors and types of regalia pay honor to these extra achievements. A bit of harmless vanity? Maybe.

British politicians at one time wore wigs to indicate their place of honor in the government and their judges still wear the wigs to reflect their special place in the government. We should be grateful American politicians wear no uniforms or special insignia. The closest thing to special insignia are small lapel pins given to members of Congress, not much fancier than the pins I used to get for perfect Sunday school attendance.

But the temptation to exercise power leadership rather than servant leadership is not restricted to people in official positions. Jesus' teaching that we should be people whose one concern is to serve is meant for every citizen. Many citizens pay little attention to government until they have a pressing need. Then instead of seeking to serve, they demand to be served. They try to throw around their weight as an individual voter to get what they want or they combine their voice with others and insist that the needs of their group be met. Isn't it good for the needs of people to be made known and for governments to seek to meet those needs? Of course. But the way of Jesus is serving, not demanding service. It is using one's influence on behalf of those who are much less fortunate. It is finding ways to meet the needs through the private sector, not sitting and waiting for the government to come to the rescue.

Early Quakers developed an unusual conviction about their behavior in the presence of public officials. The practice at the time was to remove one's hat in the presence of a king or other high official. Quakers decided that custom was contrary to the truth that all people are created by God and are of equal worth in God's sight. They felt it would be wrong to show undue respect to someone because of his position of power. And some of these Quakers ended up in jail or worse, as a result. Most Quakers today would not have a problem with being respectful toward a president or a governor, but would at the same time view those officials as servants and not deities. Citizens can either contribute to the excessive elevation of their public officials, or can learn to see these leaders as God sees them, people of no greater or lesser worth than others. Respect is always in order. Worship is not.

MEET SHARON HAYDEN

Law school was not her original plan. A social work major in college, she had dreams about bringing healing to the many ills of society. But her first jobs were not in social work; they were in retail management. It would have been sensible and secure to continue in her business career, but Sharon Hayden followed her heart into law school and passed the bar exam when she was forty years old. Now she's a public prosecutor, somewhat to her own surprise. She enjoys her career and finds plenty of opportunities to practice Christian servanthood.

Her friends in law school probably thought Sharon would take on the typical liberal causes, maybe become an ACLU lawyer. She had expressed distaste for "the system" in her law school days, so they wouldn't have predicted that Sharon would become a public prosecutor, part of the system. Her route to this career began when she selected an internship in a prosecutor's office in order to strengthen her speaking skills and her confidence in arguing cases. She found she liked the work and was good at it.

She began to realize there were good and bad law enforcement officials and good and bad prosecutors. She realized she could make the system better by becoming one of the good ones.

Sharon finds that her work is more than a job. The ministry aspect carries out the biblical mandate to "do justice." She understands this means more than assuring that wrongdoers are punished. For her, doing justice means treating a person as one God loves and one who is worthy of respect. The person's actions might be despicable, and he or she needs to be held accountable for those actions. But Sharon resists the inclination so common in her environment to treat the accused as the scum of the earth. The word that characterizes her attitude toward the accused is *redemption.* She believes that people's lives and history can be redeemed through God's power. In many cases she sees people continuing to act in predictable ways, repeating criminal behavior, stuck in a repeated pattern of violent and cruel treatment of others. But she also understands the kind of transformation that can come about; people can once again function the way God created them and intended them to be. That belief keeps her going as she deals with an unending flow of family violence cases. Her choices as a prosecutor might be a factor in someone's life being taken or spared.

Sharon has been a prosecutor long enough to realize there are no quick and simple solutions to the problems in criminal justice systems. But she enjoys letting her respect for people and her integrity rub off on young attorneys getting their first experience in the system. Her choice of career doesn't put her in the headlines very often, but she feels comfortable with her form of servanthood — serving her colleagues in the system and serving the accused and the victims in a way that nudges them toward hope and away from despair.

CHAPTER TWELVE

Loyalty to God
over Loyalty to Government

They had been able to talk their way out of the problem the first time. Call it a "plea bargain agreement" if you like. Most people would not have felt they had a problem at all. What could be wrong with eating the food and drinking the wine they were served like the others who lived in the palace? After all, they were entitled to a few privileges. These young men, called Daniel, Hananiah, Mishael, and Azariah in Hebrew, were the best of the best. They were bright, handsome, and healthy. From all the Hebrew young men in exile they were selected as those with the greatest potential to succeed in what might be called a graduate program in Babylonian language and culture. They were on the fast track to important positions in the Babylonian government.

So why should the Hebrews fuss about their daily diet in Nebuchadnezzar's palace? Wasn't the whole point of this program to do what was expected and to take advantage of this wonderful education program and open door to government service? The problem didn't seem to be with serving in the Babylonian court. Actually, we are not told exactly why Daniel became conscience-stricken about the diet in the palace. Most likely Daniel's problem with the food was that it had been offered to the temple idols before being served to the king's staff.

It looked like the four Hebrews were about to be dismissed from the Babylonian graduate school. That's when Daniel made the deal that saved them from expulsion. Fortunately, Ashpenaz, chief of staff to the king, had been impressed with the Hebrews, especially Daniel. So when Daniel came to Ashpenaz to explain that their consciences would not allow them to accept the food and drink they had been given, Ashpenaz held back on his first inclination, to toss the four men out and go look for others to take their place. Daniel came up with a "win-win" proposition. According to the agreement the two worked out, Ashpenaz expected the young men to stay in good health. If by eating other food they would still be in good physical condition, he could be flexible. The four men would also win if by eating food not offered to idols they could stay in good physical and spiritual health. It worked! The Hebrews looked great at the end of ten days, even better than the students eating the regular royal food. The four men did not have to disobey the rules of their graduate school and went ahead with their vegetarian diet for the entire three years of their studies (Daniel 1:3-21).

The second time the consciences of the four Hebrew men clashed with the rules of the Babylonian kingdom, things did not go so well. Daniel and his friends had been enjoying their training program. They made a unique contribution to their leaders by praying to God for an interpretation of one of Nebuchadnezzar's dreams. Daniel, through a direct message from Jehovah God, did what all the magicians, enchanters, sorcerers, and astrologers of Babylonia could not do. He told the king the contents of the dream, and provided it full interpretation. In doing so, Daniel gave complete credit to God. Nebuchadnezzar was impressed, not only with Daniel's abilities, but also with the God whose power Daniel evidenced. Quick and dramatic promotions followed for the Hebrews. Like Joseph before him, Daniel immediately was given the second most powerful position in the kingdom and saw to it that his three friends were given high appointments as well (Daniel 2:1-49).

Senator Mark Hatfield on loyalty to God over governments

"I do not pretend, in any way, to be a theologian; yet it seems obvious to me that Christians who, on the basis of Romans 13, look to government as a divinely instituted source of God's authority are making a grave biblical mistake, misinterpreting Scripture and harming their Christian witness. Rather, we must never lose sight of the responsibility to call government into judgment and account to see that it nurtures justice, as defined biblically. Also, as reflected in the more sound of the theological views just discussed, the Christian must always view government as part of a fallen order and as motivated by its own pretensions and striving for power. As such it must never be the final authority for the Christian; rather the revelation of Jesus Christ, and his triumph and love, must be seen as the final judge and authority over all government."[33]

For all his kind words about the Hebrew God, Nebuchadnezzar had no thought of abandoning the Babylonian gods. His magicians and astrologers had not been able to summon the power of their gods to interpret the king's dream, but they surmised that the people of the land needed to be more faithful in the worship of their gods. What better way to strengthen the worship than to erect a huge statue? You could see it for many miles across the plains around Babylonia. As people approached it, they were not sure if it was supposed to remind them of the gods or if it was meant to look like the king himself. Nebuchadnezzar probably wanted some of the worship to be directed his way as well as to the gods. Separation of religion from the government? Absolutely not! It was a two-for-one deal, worshiping the gods and the king at the same time.

What a spectacle it was when the huge statue was dedicated. The musicians signaled it was time for the worship to begin, and as far as you could see, people were bowing in reverence. This included not just Babylonians, but people of many languages and cultures who had been brought as captives to the city or were there doing business. All the officials had been coached that they were to lead the way in this massive service of prayer and praise to the pagan gods and their king. But wait a minute! Some of the Babylonian astrologers who were supposed to be bowing in prayer were actually looking around among the officials and could not spot Daniel and his friends anywhere. Keep in mind that these were the same advisors whose lives had been spared because of the dream interpretation God had provided through Daniel. Why were they counting noses when they should have been praying? Why wouldn't they have been willing to keep their mouths shut, since they owed their lives to the four Hebrews?

Call it racism, if you wish. These Babylonians had been embarrassed that they were not able to tell what the king's dream was, much less what it meant. Now these foreigners were their bosses! And it was obvious to anyone who had spent time at the court that the Hebrews had remained loyal to the Hebrew God. So a mixture of jealousy and anger motivated the king's officials once they had verified that the Hebrews hadn't been bowing down to the statue that day. They echoed the rage of the royal officials in the time of the Persian king Xerxes. He complained that the Hebrews had customs that were "different from those of all other people, and they do not obey the king's laws; it is not in the king's best interest to tolerate them" (Esther 3:8).

Clearly, all four of the Hebrews had been conspicuous by their absence during the worship ceremonies for the gods and the king. But the conspirators did not want to push their luck by including Daniel, the next most powerful man in the land, in their accusations. Instead they accused only the three friends, who now had Babylonian names, Shadrach, Meshach, and Abednego.

Who should Nebuchadnezzar have believed? The astrologers who couldn't interpret his dreams or the Hebrews whom he had given places of high honor in the land? The exchange between the king and the accused was very interesting. He asked the men if it was true that they had not worshiped the statue. Without wait-

**William Wilberforce on the object
of the Christian's allegiance**

"Another principle of the true Christian is that he recognizes this
world is not his resting place. Here to the very last, he must be
a pilgrim and a stranger. He is a soldier, whose welfare ends
only with life. He is ever struggling and combating with the
powers of darkness, and the temptations of the world around
him, and the still more dangerous hostilities of inward
sinfulness."[34]

ing for an answer, he decided to give them a second chance.
Maybe they had been involved in some important matters of state
when the call to prayer sounded. Maybe they had not quite
grasped the importance of the order or had not understood that
the threat of being thrown into a hot furnace was real. If the king
made the situation a little clearer to them, they would probably go
along with the order and he wouldn't have to punish them. When
the king finally gave them a chance to speak, it was not long before he realized there was no misunderstanding at all. They knew
they were supposed to show up at the prayer meeting, but they
deliberately skipped out on it. The king had probably never found
out about their special diet. Now they left no doubt about their
loyalties:

> "O Nebuchadnezzar, we do not need to defend ourselves be-
> fore you in this matter. If we are thrown into the blazing fur-
> nace, the God we serve is able to save us from it, and he will
> rescue us from your hand, O king. But even if he does not, we
> want you to know, O king, that we will not serve your gods or
> worship the image of gold you have set up."

*Hey, were you guys sleeping during your graduate school classes
when the professors taught about being respectful and obedient? What
made you think you could stand there and tell the king to his face that
you weren't going to follow his orders to worship the statue?* We know
the rest of the story very well. About heating the furnace seven

times hotter than before. About the absurdity of tying up the Hebrews before tossing them in. About the unfortunate soldiers who lost their lives from the intense heat as they were throwing the Hebrews into the fire. And especially about what seems from the account in Daniel to have been Jesus or an angel walking with the Hebrews in the furnace (Daniel 3:1-27).

King Nebuchadnezzar himself most accurately characterized this amazing example of civil disobedience:

> "Praise be to the God of Shadrach, Meshach, and Abednego,
> who has sent his angel and rescued his servants! They trusted
> in him and defied the king's command, and were willing to
> give up their lives rather than serve or worship any god except
> their own God." (Daniel 3:28)

What are we to learn from this account as citizens and followers of Christ—that it doesn't matter if we are obedient to civil authorities? To teach that would be to clash with a number of biblical teachings, especially the strong messages in Romans 13 about submitting to governmental authorities. But the New Testament grounds for civil disobedience echo the passage in Daniel. In one of the most striking, in Acts 4, the situation is similar to the one in Babylon. To obey the civil authorities would have meant disobeying God. Peter and John could not stop talking about Jesus and would not soften their harsh words about those who rejected and executed Jesus.

The apostles had been warned before, but refused to walk away in silence. Like the three Hebrews standing before the king who had the power to take their lives, Peter and John made their loyalties absolutely clear:

> "Judge for yourselves whether it is right in God's sight to obey
> you rather than God. For we cannot help speaking about what
> we have seen and heard." (Acts 4:19-20)

Some conservative Christians are uncomfortable with the phrase, "civil disobedience." They might be called "Romans 13 Christians," who emphasize the biblical teaching on submission and obedience. They think of government as an instrument of God, as Romans 13:1 says. But the passages from Daniel and Acts are clearly cases of God-directed civil disobedience. One should think of them primarily as God-obedience, more than civil disobedience. In many cases there is no clash between obeying God and the government. But sometimes it simply is not possible to avoid the clash; obedience to God requires disobedience to the government.

These principles are consistent with the teaching of Scripture:

✓ **Loyalty to God is the one absolute for the follower of Christ.** Time after time the Bible, especially the Old Testament, makes clear that there is a covenant given to the people of God. Simply put, the covenant declares that obeying God releases God's blessings; disobeying God brings horrible consequences to the disobedient.

✓ Depending on the kind of government of which we are citizens, **we can be respectful, obedient, and loyal to our government much of the time.** And depending on the extent to which that government is responsive to the voice of citizens, we may have opportunities to influence the government in positive ways.

✓ In some cases, **obedience to God may clash with the direct orders we receive from government officials,** but negotiations may be possible to alter the circumstances and permit obedience to both the government and our God. The four Hebrews were able to arrange for a new diet that would not violate their consciences.

✓ **In other cases, there is no middle ground** and obedience to God requires disobedience to the government. The three Hebrews were given an ultimatum to worship the statue of the pagan god and the king. There was no middle ground. They could not partially serve the pagan gods and partially serve Jehovah God.

✓ The Hebrews and Peter and John explained their plans for **civil disobedience in a courageous, respectful, loving manner.** They were not hostile, defiant, and angry. You might even say they expressed love toward the officials who were threatening them. They acted in keeping with Titus 3:2, "to slander no one, to be peaceable and considerate, and to show true humility toward all men." But they were not able to do what the preceding verse says, "to be subject to rulers and authorities, to be obedient." Respectful, yes. Obedient, no.

✓ Shadrach, Meshach, and Abednego on the one hand, and Peter and John on the other hand, were quite willing to **accept the consequences of their disobedience.** They made it very clear they knew that the consequences of their disobedience could be death. They were not seeking martyrdom for its own sake, but they also were not trying to escape the consequences of their actions. The Hebrews accurately predicted that God would deliver them, but said they would not act any differently if they knew God would not rescue them.

✓ Civil disobedience in these biblical cases was **not a tactic to gain publicity and generate support for a movement.** Nor was it a device to embarrass the government for punishing innocent people. The disobedience was fully based on convictions. The ultimatums of the governments gave no choice apart from disobedience.

MEET BEV DAVENPORT

A piece of mail stood out among the day's offers of credit cards and "free" trips to Las Vegas. This piece of mail didn't contain any offers or opportunities. It was very official looking: "You are hereby summoned to appear for jury duty in the circuit court." It ended with sentences that were meant to motivate the reluctant: "Please do not fail to respond. Although jury service may be an inconvenience, it can also be an opportunity to participate in an important civic duty. After serving, most jurors report that the experience was a positive one. Your full participation is expected."

The recipient of this jury summons would describe herself as an average person. She is a wife, mother, and grandmother, someone without special expertise in civic participation, but someone who seeks to serve Christ in the opportunities that come to her. Many people view jury duty as a nuisance, a disruption of their work schedules and their family responsibilities. Some of them ask for exemption, and the law does allow for this. When Bev Davenport received her jury summons, she had no thought of asking to be excused from serving even though she was uneasy about what might lie ahead. She wondered if her Christian convictions would clash with her duties as a juror, but felt participating was not only a civic duty, but was part of being a faithful follower of Christ. She knew no Scriptures that talked about jury duty, but thought the passages about paying taxes were relevant. She felt it was both her Christian and public duty to do what she could to make the judicial system work, even when it might have some flaws.

Bev felt, when she and other potential jurors were shown into the courtroom, that this was an important and serious undertaking. She had seen television shows centered in the courtroom, but this was real. A plaintiff sought damages for his renter's alleged breach of contract and it was up to a group of randomly selected individuals to determine what was right and fair. No one would go to jail or be tainted by a criminal charge, but serious financial consequences would follow the jury's decision.

Being part of the legal process fascinated Bev since she had no legal training or previous court experience. She enjoyed getting acquainted with other jurors and discovering how differently the jurors interpreted the same testimony and evidence. She came to realize that reasonable people, even Christian people, could arrive at opposite conclusions based on what they saw and heard. The most rewarding part of the process was discovering that her lack of specialized training did not stand in the way of her contributing to the group's decision making. Others in the jury had more experience than she did in working with official documents, but she noticed and explained something the other jurors had overlooked. In doing so, she contributed to the jury's ability to agree on a decision they felt was right.

Bev was relieved that her jury dealt with a civil case, not a criminal case. She didn't like the idea of being part of a decision that would result in a heavy jail sentence. But she had a positive experience and feels she might be less reluctant about involvement in a criminal case if she were summoned again. She considers her time on the jury as an excellent learning experience and as an opportunity to understand some of the strengths and weaknesses of the court system. She has a greater understanding of the stress involved for those who are parties in a case and for the witnesses. She has a greater appreciation for judges, court officers, and attorneys who deal with many cases a day and cannot walk away like the jurors when they are dismissed. Bev performed an important function as an active Christian citizen and has some pleasant memories from having done so.

CHAPTER THIRTEEN

Influencing Public Decision-Makers

It was not a good time to be a women's liberationist. Queen Vashti had had her fill of being the king's sex object, of being paraded before the king's guests to impress them with her beauty, her elaborate clothes, and her crown. No one else in the king's court understood Vashti's feelings. What were queens for, anyway, if not to show the king's great taste in women? They were to come when called, to show off their beauty, and to make the king proud.

To the complete shock of the servants sent to bring Vashti to King Xerxes, she did not drop what she was doing and come as the king had requested. She told the attendants she would not leave the guests at her own banquet to go and be shown off as the king's prize possession.

"Not coming! What do you mean, not coming?" bellowed the king in a rage. What a horrible embarrassment to have a banquet hall full of the most important men in the kingdom and to be told the queen would not come to pay them a visit. The king gathered his legal experts and top advisors around to help him decide what to do about the terrible affront.

Memucan, the senior advisor, spoke for the others. "King Xerxes, the laws of the land are very clear on this matter. Vashti cannot remain as queen when she has completely defied your request. We know you have admired her very much, but you have to replace her as queen. There is no need to put her to death, just send her out of the palace and find a new queen. It's not just the concern about upholding the law; Vashti's defiance is a threat to the entire social order. Since everyone in the realm will hear about Vashti's rebellious actions, all the women will stop obeying their husbands. This is huge. Our society might not survive the chaos that would result from women refusing to stay in their place" (paraphrase of Esther 1:16-22).

Memucan need not have worried about King Xerxes getting the point; he was furious. He sent Vashti packing and simultaneously sent out an order that the women in the kingdom should take warning from Vashti's fate and must continue to be faithful and loyal to their husbands. In short order, the king set in motion the search for a new queen. The requirements for the queen were simple: She must be charming, poised, and beautiful—above all, beautiful. There was no talent competition for the "Miss Persia" contest; the winner needed only a gorgeous face and a stunning body. Many entered the contest but there was a little-known fact about the winner. A Hebrew, she was a descendant of the Jews who had been brought as captives from Judah. Perhaps her Jewish features made her even more attractive to the king than the local women. And a year of beauty treatments made her even more irresistible.

The entrance of Esther into the royal household and her crowning as queen brought into the story another Jew, her cousin and adoptive father, Mordecai. Mordecai's love and protection had spared the life of this orphan girl. And on Mordecai's advice Esther did not reveal her ancestry while she lived in the harem and after she became queen. From the time Esther had been rounded up by the king's beauty scouts, Mordecai did his best to assure her safety and well-being. Every day he went to the palace to ask if she was all right.

Mordecai spent much of the rest of his days near the king's gate, the place political information was most available. There he hoped to pick up some news from the royal household and there

Senator Mark Hatfield on influencing government

"There is an old saying, 'All that is necessary for evil to triumph is for good men to do nothing.' This is precisely where we find ourselves today in the matter of Christian ethics and political morality. For many political generations too many good men have done nothing. They have stood by as neutral observers while the contest was fought in the political arena. This is true in the local community, it is widespread on the state level, and it is certainly the case in national politics.

"If the message of the transforming power of God in Christ is applicable to the individual human being, then it must have an effect upon social man and his community. A man's view of the world and his relationships to those around him must change when he is confronted with the message of the gospel. Changed men must build a changed world. Christians must become involved in the processes of transformation in our world as God leads them. One of the major processes for orderly change in our world is politics—the art and science of human government."[35]

he heard the news of Esther's choice as queen. At the gates one could gather information and possibly influence public life. Mordecai's first experience at the gates turned out to be very important in his future well-being, but at the time it passed with little notice. In the gates, Mordecai heard two of the king's staff members plotting to kill the king. He had no reason not to be loyal to the king, so he sent word of the plot through Esther to the king. In reporting it, Esther was careful to give Mordecai the credit for the information that brought an end to the plot. The episode ended with a public hanging, with the two plotters executed for their treason. Palace historians recorded the event and gave appropriate credit to Mordecai.

Mordecai's next experience at the king's gate did not go as well. The king had promoted one of his staff members, Haman, to a position just below the king. Part of the protocol for such a high official required that all the subjects of the realm bow down before him. Haman liked this part of his new position. He loved the fine clothes he was entitled to wear and he thoroughly enjoyed seeing people scramble before him to pay respect. That's how Mordecai got in trouble. We are not told in the book of Esther exactly why Mordecai would not bow before Haman. It was not just an oversight, for the king's staff kept reminding him what he was supposed to do. They warned him they would have to report him, but he would not listen. It could be that Haman was asking for more than the normal respect Jews were willing to give to the rulers in their land of exile. Haman, it seems, was asking the people to worship him and Mordecai knew there was only one he could worship, Jehovah God.

Haman, hateful and bigoted, was not content with making Mordecai suffer for his unwillingness to bow down. Haman had learned that Mordecai was a Jew and he insanely decided that all Jews should die for the impertinence of one. He set in motion what could have become the first Jewish holocaust. Haman, a clever man, had figured out how to get the king to do what he wanted. Instead of telling Xerxes he wanted all the Jews killed, Haman fabricated a story about the disloyalty of the Jews. He purposely avoided telling the king who these people were before the king issued the order for their extermination. Haman probably knew Esther was Jewish, knowing that Mordecai was her relative. Haman even offered a huge bribe to assure that the king would issue the order for the annihilation of the Jews.

Fortunately for Esther, Mordecai, and their fellow Jews, the death sentence did not take effect immediately. In fact, Esther did not even hear about it for a while. Her staff learned that Mordecai was back at the king's gate, this time in deep mourning, wearing the traditional clothes of grief, made of sackcloth. A series of messages went back and forth between Mordecai and Esther, explaining the reason for his mourning and giving details of the planned execution. Then Mordecai sent a message that presented a huge

William Wilberforce on influencing government

"Acting on these principles, the true Christian will studiously and diligently use any degree of worldly reputation he may enjoy in removing or lessening prejudices. He will use it to conciliate good will and thereby make way for the less obstructive progress of truth. Providing it entertains him with candor or even with favor, he will make it his business to step forward with benevolent and useful schemes. And where it requires united efforts to obtain and preserve it, he will seek the cooperation of men of good will."[36]

problem for Esther. He asked that she use her position as queen to plead for mercy for the Jews. The messages continued, Esther explaining that a king who would depose his queen for disobedience would do even worse for a queen who went to see him without an invitation. He would have her killed. The exchange of messages continued. Mordecai argued that the risk of death for disobeying the rules of the palace was no greater than the prospect of Esther's nationality becoming known. Then she would be killed with all the other Jews (Esther 4:1-17).

Esther had a huge decision to make. She sent word back to Mordecai to have all the Jews join in fasting and prayer that Esther would have clarity of thought and courage. She decided in that time of prayer to go ahead and risk her life in the hope of saving her people. She also decided on the tactic of making a request the king could not refuse, that he and his top official, Haman, come to a banquet in their honor. The tactic worked. The king was so impressed with Esther's graciousness he offered her half his kingdom. She declined the offer and asked only that he and Haman come to another banquet in their honor. What an amazing thing, they both thought. This beautiful queen could have asked for many things, but she was so humble she asked only that they come to another dinner.

Meanwhile, back at the king's gates, Mordecai had another run-in with the arrogant Haman. It was not enough that Haman had been one of only two honored guests of the queen. It was not enough that he could have received almost anything he wanted in the kingdom. But it annoyed him greatly to see Mordecai sitting there in the gates, still mourning about the fate of the Jews, and still refusing to humble himself before Haman. He was so angry, he almost ordered his attendants to kill Mordecai on the spot. If not for the king's order that would soon take Mordecai's life along with the rest of the Jews, Haman would probably have killed Mordecai that day at the king's gate. But he bit his tongue and hurried home to complain to his wife about the impertinent Mordecai and to brag about being the queen's honored guest.

Behind this vain and arrogant man was an evil woman, reinforcing his anger and spite, urging him to carry out his hateful actions. Haman's wife, Zaresh, was the source of the plan for dealing with Mordecai. It would be appropriate, reasoned Zaresh, to have Mordecai hanged from huge gallows, for all to see. It would help the Jews to understand their status as distrusted minorities. Surely with as much favor as Haman had with the king and queen, he could get approval for the hanging.

Historians can find in the next part of the story how important their vocation is. The court historian had carefully recorded the case of Mordecai reporting the plot against the king. To cure his insomnia, Xerxes had the court history book read to him during the night between the two banquets. To his chagrin, he discovered that nothing had been done to reward Mordecai. That did not seem right to Xerxes; he owed his life to this man who spent his days in the city gates.

The next scene in this story is amusing to readers today, but its outcome was not at all amusing to Haman. Unfortunately, Haman happened to be nearby in the palace when Xerxes was trying to think of an appropriate way to honor Mordecai. And unfortunately for Haman, Xerxes asked for Haman's ideas for honoring an important person, without saying Mordecai was the one to be honored. Haman's egotism kicked in and he could not imagine there would be anyone besides himself the king would want to honor. So he stretched the limits of the normal protocol for dispensing honors. He proposed that the honored person be allowed to wear one of the king's own royal robes and be allowed to ride one of the king's own horses through the city. To make it clear that this person was very special in the king's eyes, one of the high officials of the land was to lead the horse, proclaiming to everyone what a great person this was.

Zaresh would have been proud of her husband's cleverness in asking for such extraordinary recognition. And then the other shoe dropped. Put yourself in Haman's place. You were savoring the moment of high honor, being paraded through the streets with everyone cheering. And then the king tells you that you are the one to lead the horse and do the proclaiming, not to ride the horse. Either Xerxes was clueless about Haman's intense hatred for Mordecai or he had a great sense of humor. What could be more humiliating than to lead the royal horse bearing your worst enemy through the streets, shouting that he was a person of great honor in the king's eyes? Haman thought he was just hours away from being able to "lift up" Mordecai to die on the gallows and instead he had to be the one to lift up Mordecai in honor before the people. What an amazing turn of events! And it did not help that when Haman's wife and staff members heard what a miserable day he had, they predicted he would never prevail against the God-fearing Mordecai (Esther 6).

Esther's second banquet for the king and Haman had a different outcome from the first one. Once again the food and wine were the finest available. Once again Esther's charm and beauty made Xerxes eager to please her and grant her requests. But it was obvious that Haman had not had a good day. It was not what he said, but what he did not say. He was not jumping into the conversation to talk about his great achievements as the king's top official. He was visibly nervous, for good reason.

In the time it took for a few short sentences to come from Esther's mouth, Haman's bright future was ended and the first step had been taken toward ending the horrible sentence against all the Jews in Persia. Xerxes had a habit of losing his temper when confronted with disturbing new information. He loved his beautiful new queen and she was now telling him that she was a Jew and that she would soon lose her life, along with all the other Hebrews in the kingdom. Xerxes should have known this would be one of the outcomes when he first issued the execution order. He seems to have been oblivious to a good bit of what was happening around him. Esther knew about his emotional volatility and how to plan the telling of her story so as to take full advantage of his inevitable outbursts of anger. Who could have come up with the idea of such a cruel order to kill the Jews? Look across the table, King Xerxes. It's one of the guests at dinner and there are only three of us here.

For a man who knew he was an inch away from losing his life, Haman did not play his cards very well while the king paced in the garden considering his options. Haman, who had always been able to talk his way out of a jam, fell down before Esther to plead for mercy. *Not a smart thing to do, Haman. What if the king should return and misinterpret your actions?* The worst happened, as far as Haman was concerned. Xerxes returned to the banquet room and concluded that Haman was either trying to seduce Esther or to threaten her physically. Unfortunately for Haman, the king's staff knew about some new gallows Haman had built for Mordecai. Haman was planning to ride through the cities in honor and then to have Mordecai hanged. Instead, Mordecai rode through the city and Haman was hanged.

Mordecai's life had been like a roller coaster. One day he was grieving in sackcloth for the possible death of all Jews in exile. The next day he was being paraded through the city in Persia's version of a ticker tape parade. The next day the enemy of his people was gone and he was invited into the palace to receive Haman's estate and the signet ring symbolizing the king's great power. And that same day the king directed Mordecai to write the order reversing the death sentence on Jews. With the same ring Haman had used to seal the death order, Mordecai sent out the official announcement that the Jews were not to be killed. The Jews' jubilation is one of the high points in their experience of God's deliverance:

> For the Jews it was a time of happiness and joy, gladness and honor. In every province and in every city, wherever the edict of the king went, there was joy and gladness among the Jews, with feasting and celebrating. And many people of other nationalities became Jews because fear of the Jews had seized them. (Esther 8:16-17)

We may learn many lessons from the events narrated in the book of Esther. Esther is worthy of our great respect for risking her own life to plead for the safety of her people. She probably could have found a way to hide her identity as a Jew and survive the holocaust. But in some ways Mordecai was the greater hero. With respect to understanding godly citizenship, he provides a great example of a person with little power himself, who was able to work for justice through his connections with those in power.

Time after time Mordecai was able to benefit from the information he gathered by staying in touch with national affairs. He hung out at the king's gate, learned of a plot on the king's life, and received the delayed appreciation of the king. He continued to spend time at the gates, even though he knew it could be risky not to join in the near deification of Haman. And when warned by Haman's staff that he must participate in the worship of Haman, he refused. Then he headed back to the gates to publicly mourn the death sentence imposed on the Jews, choosing not to express his grief in the relative safety of the Jewish quarter. Maybe Mordecai could have escaped the Jews' fate by asking for Esther's protection, but he accepted the risks of using his relationship with Esther to talk her into intervening with the king. Even while these delicate negotiations were under way, Mordecai took one more serious risk by refusing to bow down to Haman.

In some ways Mordecai was like those who work for interest groups in seeking to influence the government. He kept informed on political events and knew how to use his connections toward important ends. He encouraged Esther to become a part of the king's household and used his family ties to gain access to power and ultimately to set in motion the deliverance of the entire Jewish population.

Those who play the Mordecai role among the citizenry in American politics today have learned how to use their knowledge and their contacts to advance many important causes in their government. Among those methods of the modern Mordecai are these:

- ✓ **Staying spiritually grounded, to be ready to respond to crises that suddenly arise.** For some reason, the book of Esther does not speak directly about the relationship Mordecai and Esther had with Jehovah God. It does mention Esther's call to fasting when she was preparing to talk with the king. The Hebrews' practice of fasting was one of their methods of praying for God's help. This was not just a time of skipping meals, but it was the kind of fasting described in Isaiah 58, "Is not this the kind of fasting…to loose the chains of injustice and untie the cords of the yoke, to set the oppressed free and break every yoke?" Mordecai might have been aware of passages in the Scripture like the one in Isaiah, imploring him "not to turn away from your own flesh and blood" (Isaiah 58:6-7).

- ✓ **To stay well informed about national events and issues.** For Mordecai this meant spending significant amounts of time at the king's gates where those close to the palace talked about what was going on there. Today's Mordecais have the media and Internet sources of information.

- ✓ **To carefully use one's political connections.** As a non-Persian, Mordecai did not have any political connections until the amazing turn of events that put his adopted daughter into the palace. Modern Mordecais may feel they don't know anyone in power, but those who are concerned Christian citizens should be alert for opportunities to meet well-placed leaders and to build relationships with them, ranging from casual acquaintance to trusted friendships.

✓ **To take a courageous stand for justice and truth.** Esther was not at all sure at first if she should risk her life to defend her people. Mordecai's courage inspired her and brought her to the point of saying, "If I perish, I perish" (Esther 4:16). The stories of people who have accomplished great things frequently contain events that tested their strength and courage. They have had to decide if the stand they were taking was worthy of death. Mordecai took such a stand. So did Esther. Many others have since.

MEET MARIE RIETMAN

She grew up on a large wheat ranch near Condon, Oregon, a ways up the road from Fossil and further from Antelope. Being a rancher's daughter meant helping with herding the cattle, spending time running the combine, and taking her turn on the tractor. It meant being active in 4-H and learning about agriculture and about leadership. Being a member of her family meant exposure to public policy issues, since her father was the local contact for Senator Mark Hatfield. When it was time for a reelection campaign or when the senator was ready to come to Gilliam County to touch base with his constituents, the senator's staff called her father.

Marie Rietman's heritage of agriculture and politics shows up throughout two decades spent on both sides of the political process, as a congressional staff member and a lobbyist. She received a degree in agriculture from Oregon State University. While a student, she spent time with the Oregon legislature as a page. Later she worked for Oregon House of Representatives member Tony Van Vliet and was on Senator Hatfield's staff in his Oregon offices. She also served as a staff member for two of Oregon's U.S. representatives, Elizabeth Furse and Earl Blumenauer, in Washington, D.C.

It is often the case that Oregon wheat ranchers are conservative in their political views. But Marie has worked for members of Congress with decidedly liberal views, especially on international issues. She has helped them pursue such issues as the nuclear test ban, a ban on low yield nuclear weapons, the cleanup of unexploded ordnance, and reduced spending for unneeded items in military budgets. She has worked with private advocacy groups on these issues and others as well, including ending nuclear testing and expanding assistance to the underdeveloped world.

But Marie has not left behind her understanding of the challenges of growing wheat and finding viable markets for this important crop. She has worked for a wheat market development organization and helped prepare for discussion in Congress on strengthened marketing efforts for U.S. agricultural products abroad. Her knowledge of the wheat industry and her advocacy for more positive relationships with countries thought to be enemies of the United States connected when she organized the shipment of 200 tons of wheat to Nicaragua in the late 1980s.

Marie has lobbied members of Congress on issues important to her values and as a staff member has been lobbied as well. Experience with both sides of this process has helped her understand that effectively influencing policy issues requires developing relationships, building trust, and establishing one's credibility. She has seen good and bad examples of advocacy and tries to help those with less experience find ways to present information and arguments in ways that will impact the policy-makers. But she's been working at the process long enough to know that an almost inevitable inertia impacts some issues, and there are few quick successes. She takes comfort in Mother Teresa's reminder that we are called to be faithful, not necessarily successful.

CHAPTER FOURTEEN

Influencing Government from Within

The political setting mirrored that of Mordecai; the period of time during the exile of the Jews was similar. The same dynasty ruled. Mordecai had dealt with King Xerxes and now his son Artaxerxes sat on the throne. But there were differences between Mordecai and Nehemiah. We can attribute part of this difference to the style of the biblical accounts describing them. The book of Esther is vague about the spiritual life of the key characters; the book of Nehemiah, on the other hand, is filled with the powerful prayers of the wonderfully godly man Nehemiah. Nehemiah represents a different position from which a person might influence government. Mordecai was an outsider, only able to access the government through Esther. Nehemiah served within the Persian government. Mordecai struggled for the survival of the Jews in Persia; Nehemiah dealt with the spiritual and physical well-being of the remaining Jews who had not been deported to Persia.

To modern readers the position of cupbearer to the king might not seem all that impressive. If we checked over the staff list for the White House, we probably would not find a cupbearer anywhere. But Nehemiah had an important and hazardous job. The hazardous part shows up in the story of Joseph in Egypt. After landing in jail for false accusations of seducing the wife of one of the king's high officials, Joseph was joined there by the king's cupbearer and the king's baker. The account in Genesis does not tell what offense had landed the cupbearer in jail, but this person's job included tasting all the king's wine and other beverages to be sure some enemy of the king had not poisoned his drinks. Joseph's fellow prisoner had not poisoned the pharaoh in Egypt. Maybe the king simply did not like the wine that day. Or maybe the cupbearer had abused his position of trust by "leaking" an unflattering story about the king.

Nehemiah's job as cupbearer assured the safety and well-being of Artaxerxes. That put him among a handful of individuals who had the king's trust and who had the most consistent access to the king. He would have been carefully chosen for his absolute integrity and perhaps like Daniel and his friends, being Hebrew might have had some appeal to Artaxerxes. Nehemiah was not likely to be part of the plotting that might be under way to remove the king from power.

Actually the plotting and planning was happening back in Judah, where the Jews who had not been deported and others who had returned from Persia had been at work rebuilding the temple. Oddly enough, this work was being done with the specific permission of one of Artaxerxes' predecessors a century before, King Cyrus. Rebuilding the temple was one thing, but the Jews then turned to a broader agenda of rebuilding the rest of the city and its walls. These more ambitious plans agitated Artaxerxes' representatives in Judah. They sent a letter to the king, warning that the rebuilding activity would undermine Persian power in Judah. Their letter was filled with propaganda and misrepresentation, labeling Jerusalem as a hotbed of rebellion, trouble, and wickedness. Without giving any solid evidence for their case, these on-site officials argued that the rebuilding of Jerusalem would stop the flow of taxes and tribute to Persia. The king's power in Judah would be finished (Ezra 4:6-16).

The letter to Artaxerxes worked. The king sent his staff to dig back into the royal archives and based on the information provided by his staff decided the description of Jerusalem as a hotbed of rebellion and sedition was accurate. The enemies of the Jews had their way. The king immediately ordered that the rebuilding cease and it did. Artaxerxes accepted the argument that this was much more than an effort of the Jews to strengthen their worship. It was intended to weaken and eliminate Persian control in Judah (Ezra 4:17-24).

Nehemiah was not one to stay inside the comfort and security of the Persian palace. He cared about the Jews and went regularly to the Jewish quarter in Persepolis, the Persian capital, to get the news about the Jews in Persia and in Judah. The book of Nehemiah begins with such a visit, an account of Nehemiah talking with fellow Jews about the news "at home" in Judah. The news was not good. The strong opposition of the Persian provincial officials and the support of Artaxerxes had ended the rebuilding efforts. The Jews were discouraged. Hope had died (Nehemiah 1:1-3).

Nehemiah was devastated by the bad news from Judah. He apparently took a leave of absence from his duties at the palace, for the account says he spent days fasting, praying, and mourning for those in his home country whose desires to rebuild had been thwarted. One of Nehemiah's prayers during this time is preserved for us and is a powerful example of praise, confession, and the remembrance of God's covenant. The prayer ends with this stirring statement:

> "O Lord, let your ear be attentive to the prayer of this your
> servant and to the prayer of your servants who delight in re-
> vering your name. Give your servant success today by granting
> him favor in the presence of this man." (Nehemiah 1:11)

The reference to "this man" shows the extent to which Nehemiah moved from sadness about the condition of his homeland to the recognition that he himself had a personal obligation and calling to do something about the problems in Judah. Like Mordecai, he could have isolated himself within the walls of the palace and stifled his concerns about the Jews. But like Mordecai, Nehemiah concluded he must do something. And he knew he was in a position to actually make a difference. His was not a policy position. He was not one of the king's top advisors on the issues of the day. But it was clear he was the king's friend and the position represented an opportunity and an obligation. His days of prayer brought him to the realization that he must do something.

Nehemiah knew enough about imperial politics to know that doing something about meeting the needs in Judah would not be easy. He knew about the correspondence from the provincial officials in Jerusalem and the force behind the king's order that the rebuilding must stop. He heard plenty of conversations in the palace and he knew that the king felt strongly about this. The smart thing would have been to forget what he had heard in the Jewish quarter and squelch his interest in changing the status quo in the homeland. But when Nehemiah returned to work in the palace, he made no effort to hide his sadness about the sad state of affairs in Judah.

There are some things to admire about King Artaxerxes. One was his awareness of the state of mind of his staff members. When Nehemiah returned to work, the king saw that something was bothering him and realized it was something extremely important. Like Esther, Nehemiah was troubled about the implications of being completely open with the king about his distress. Like Esther, Nehemiah knew he would be asking for something completely contrary to a recent order of the king. Like Esther, Nehemiah felt he had the king's trust, but knew the extent to which he was going against the grain in the imperial palace. Unlike Esther, Nehemiah immediately got to the point. He had finished his prayer retreat and was ready to go deal with the issue.

God had previously performed a miracle in making King Cyrus amenable to the rebuilding of the temple in Jerusalem and in this case Artaxerxes' complete cooperation with Nehemiah's concern for Jerusalem was also amazing. Not only was Nehemiah asking that the order to stop all rebuilding be rescinded, but he was also asking for a leave of absence to go oversee the rebuilding project. Nehemiah did not stop there. He asked for letters of safe conduct for the trip, knowing very well that the Persian officials in Jerusalem and their surrounding allies would do everything possi-

Senator Mark Hatfield on public service

"The citizen-Christian, then, faces a twofold challenge. First, by obedience to the Great Commission, the teaching of the gospel of Christ, he must redeem the citizens of our society and thereby build a better foundation for government. His second challenge is to be willing to serve God in politics and government if that is where God wants him. The great experiment that is America calls to each generation for the kind of men and women who will dare to make this nation what it is meant to be. The call is to service, to loyalty, to sacrifice, and to opportunity. The crisis is in the dearth of leadership. The greatest need of our times is for men who will give of themselves and who will serve unselfishly in a position of public trust. The call is for leaders who will be led by God."[37]

ble to undermine Nehemiah's mission. He also asked for the authority to use the timber from the forests controlled by the Persians. This Persian king who had previously ordered that the rebuilding of Jerusalem cease not only gave Nehemiah all these things he asked, but threw in an armed escort (Nehemiah 2:1-9).

Artaxerxes' miraculous change of heart and complete cooperation with Nehemiah's rebuilding mission did not assure the success of the mission and Nehemiah understood that very well. He knew his first task was to convince the Jewish leaders in Jerusalem that it was realistic and important to resume the rebuilding process. Before he even talked with them, he did a secret nighttime inspection of the city's walls to be sure he had good information about the reconstruction process. It turned out that the Jewish leaders were not the problem. They understood the significance of the support Nehemiah had received from the king. They had to look at the mess in Jerusalem every day and were more than ready to get back to work.

But the Persian officials in Jerusalem were another matter. A trio of stubborn and nasty Persians in the city made it their job to do everything they could to block the rebuilding of Jerusalem's walls. Their names were Sanballat, Tobias, and Geshem and they were not the kind of people any of us would enjoy knowing. They probably had been instrumental in convincing the king to stop the rebuilding and had no intention of letting the work go ahead, in spite of the letters from Artaxerxes. They first thought Nehemiah's project was a complete joke. They knew he had a position of trust in the palace, but how did that qualify him for overseeing a huge engineering and construction effort?

Sanballat and his friends watched the early stages of rebuilding with amusement, sure that it would soon end in discouragement and failure. Then the Persians began to comment privately to one another that the work was going a lot better than they expected. Nehemiah may not have known anything about construction, but the Jews were pitching in pretty impressively. One after another the gates were restored and the walls between them were filled in. As the word got out around Judah that the work was under way, skilled builders came from every direction to help. All sorts of craftsmen pitched in and even people with no building experience, like perfume-makers, joined the work force. The restoration of the strength of Jerusalem was a great morale-builder among the Jews and even the Persian detractors had to admire the energy behind the efforts. The Persians began to wonder if the surprising success of the Jews had something to do with their passionate prayers.

When it became obvious no amount of ridicule and harassment was going to slow down the Jewish rebuilding work, the Persians began to organize armed resistance. But the Jews in Jerusalem turned out to be just as good at defense as at construction. They rallied the people to arm themselves. Some concentrated on the defense process, some continued with the building, and others held weapons in one hand and construction tools in the other. Getting anything done with trowels in one hand and swords in the

William Wilberforce on the moral impact of public officials

"Circumstanced as we now are, it is more than ever obvious that the best man is the truest patriot. Nor is it by their personal conduct—though this will always be vital—that men of authority and influence may promote the cause of good works. Let them, whatever their role in society, encourage virtue and discourage vice. Let them enforce the laws which, by the wisdom of our forefathers, have guarded against the grosser infractions of morals. Let them favor and take part in any plans which may be formed for the advancement of morality. Above all things, let them endeavor to instruct and to improve the next generation."[38]

other must have been a challenge. To make sure the Jews did not get confused about the real source of their strength, Nehemiah kept reminding them God would defend them as he had done under the leadership of Gideon and numerous other Jewish leaders (Nehemiah 4:7-23).

Nehemiah might have expected that his problems would only come from Persian opposition. Not so. Next his leadership and diplomatic ability had to be directed to internal problems. The wealthy and powerful Jews had been charging exorbitant interest rates and the poor in Jerusalem had slipped deeper into poverty, had lost much of their property, and were facing near enslavement. Nehemiah was courageous and decisive in dealing with this problem. He called attention to the injustices, got the agreement of the wealthy to change their practices, and enlisted the priests in bringing spiritual pressure to bear on the Jewish nobles. Nehemiah's personal integrity and refusal to benefit financially from his leadership position helped him in making these reforms (Nehemiah 5:1-19).

Sanballat, Tobiah, and Geshem made a last attempt to block the completion of Jerusalem's walls when they could see that the project was about to be completed. They tried distracting Nehemiah by inviting him to meetings they said were important. He declined to leave his work to meet with them. They then threatened to report to the king that he was about to declare himself the king of Judah and lead the province in revolt. Nehemiah kept himself steady by remaining focused on his work and praying constantly. Finally, the trio of opponents hired a false prophet to report to Nehemiah that his life was in danger and he should go hide in the temple. He sensed this would be a contradiction to his continued trust in God and discerned that the information from the prophet was false (Nehemiah 6:1-14).

Fifty-two days from start to finish. Fifty-two days to complete something the Persians said was impossible. Fifty-two days of backbreaking labor, constant fear of enemy attack, with despair threatening to extinguish hope. Nehemiah ends his account of the project with these words of victory:

> When all our enemies heard about this and all the surrounding nations saw it, our enemies lost their self-confidence, because they realized that this work had been done with the help of our God. (Nehemiah 6:16)

The final chapter in the book of Nehemiah, after the walls of Jerusalem were dedicated, ends with the accounts of further internal problems with which Nehemiah had to deal. His prayers, interspersed in the narrative of the events, constantly expressed his trust in God, the source of his leadership strength:

> Remember me for this, O my God, and do not blot out what I have so faithfully done for the house of my God and its service.
>
> Remember me for this also, O my God, and show mercy to me according to your great love.
>
> Remember me with favor, O my God. (Nehemiah 13:14, 22, 30)

If Protestants had patron saints, Nehemiah would be the patron saint of the bureaucrats. Actually the word *bureaucrat* is loaded with negative connotations. But in neutral terms, it applies to public officials at all levels who are appointed to their offices, not elected. Like Nehemiah, some of these officials function in positions of important responsibility, but are not in the public eye most of the time. If Nehemiah had continued as cupbearer, we certainly would not have a book of the Old Testament telling his story. He might have received passing notice, like the cupbearer who briefly touched Joseph's life. But Nehemiah used his access to power to turn an obscure position into one that deeply imprinted the history of Judaism. He became a rebuilder instead of a maintainer. He was able to receive God's blessing and help in a way suggested by the prophet Isaiah:

> "You will be like a well-watered garden, like a spring whose waters never fail. Your people will rebuild the ancient ruins and will raise up the age-old foundations; you will be called Repairer of Broken Walls, Restorer of Streets with Dwellings." (Isaiah 58:11-12)

Nehemiah's example is an inspiration to appointed officials—city managers, county commissioners, legislative directors for members of Congress, deputy sheriffs, district attorneys, assistant secretaries of state, ambassadors, fire chiefs, and detectives. His example is powerful in these and many other ways:

✓ **From beginning to end, the power of his work came from his extraordinary prayer life.** The terrible tragedy of his people overwhelmed him at first, until he was able to focus on God's power and until he could picture himself taking the first step, talking to the king. He prayed when his opponents sought to undermine his work, when his own people became discouraged, when he was wrongly accused, and when his strength was gone. When the work was all done, he directed praises to God who had made it all possible.

✓ **Nehemiah used the small influence he had to access the resources of a great empire to achieve God's work.** Who would have thought that the king of a huge empire would change his position on a major foreign policy question when asked by a relatively minor member of his staff? The project could not have succeeded without the king's support. It looked like it would be impossible to gain that backing, but Nehemiah accomplished his greatest victory when he convinced the king this was the right thing for him to do.

✓ **Nehemiah had extraordinary tenacity and persistence in the face of great obstacles.** Public officials deal with tough issues at times and may often wish they had stayed in private life. Like Nehemiah, they might not be paid much and might be criticized regularly. They face opposition from within the government and from the government's opponents. Nehemiah never lost sight of his calling or looked away from his goal.

✓ **Nehemiah never confused the importance of his own efforts with the essential power of God working through him.** Elected officials have a way of becoming arrogant. Sometimes appointed officials can be even more arrogant, since they aren't directly accountable to the voters. It would have been understandable if Nehemiah had stood back from the wall construction from time to time, smiled, and thought what a great job he was doing. He probably got a lot of satisfaction from the progress on the work, but there is no hint in the Scriptures that he took the credit himself. He had not the slightest doubt that everything he accomplished was through God's power working in him. *Way to go, Nehemiah! We're impressed.*

MEET DAVE BISHOP

You might call him a "bureaucrat," for much of his working career has been in positions that are appointed rather than elected. But he might prefer to be called a public servant, not just accountable to the voters at the next election, but to some higher ideals of meeting human needs with public resources. He remembers that while he was growing up a family friend encouraged him to develop his gifts for leadership and that experience planted the seed in his mind that his avenue of service might be within the government. His name is Dave Bishop and he manages the operations of one part of Oregon's Department of Transportation. His agency builds and maintains roads, but he prefers to think of his work as finding effective solutions for community needs so that members of that community can live peaceful and productive lives.

Dave's choice of majors and courses at Seattle Pacific University was intentionally broad, to provide a foundation for public service. He studied business administration, economics, and political science, then went on for a master's degree in urban planning. With this preparation, he served two counties in Oregon in their planning and development agencies. He helped translate a new state land use law into specific local decisions about urban growth boundaries, allowing growth in suitable areas, and preventing growth that might destroy farmland, wetlands, and scenic areas. He found that most people will support these broad goals in general, but many will do everything they can to prevent the new policies from limiting their options for making money from selling or developing their own property. Those issues continued to be prominent during Dave's interval in elective office, as a county commissioner in Oregon.

Dave received mixed messages while growing up in a Christian home and attending a Christian college. On the one hand he was affirmed for his leadership abilities and accomplishments, but on the other hand he did not find many who saw a career in government service as a form of "full-time Christian service." He heard many messages about serving Christ in missions and the ministry, but not about serving Christ in full-time Christian citizenship.

Dave feels there are numerous opportunities for Christian service in his state's transportation agency. He knows there are other Christians in the department and feels that together they can help to keep the agency focused on its mission of serving people's needs. He is aware that corresponding agencies in some states have descended into corruption, since the business survival of so many contractors depends on continuing to get their share of state contracts. In those states, payoffs have been the means of gaining contracts, rather than building a strong reputation from excellent, cost-effective work.

The life and teachings of Jesus increasingly shape Dave's ideals and practices as a state agency administrator. Jesus regularly challenged the defenders of the status quo; he often took the side of the weaker members of the community when the wealthy and powerful wanted things to stay as they were. Dave sees Jesus as a nurturer of the community rather than the defender of individual freedom. Dave's work with land issues at the county level prepared him well for the controversies that surround his work on transportation projects. Motorists, business owners, property owners, and community members often become enemies of one another rather than collaborating on mutually beneficial solutions. Dave seeks to be a mediator and reconciler among these interests, hoping to find solutions that are win/win, rather than win/lose.

CHAPTER FIFTEEN

Doing God's Work
in the Public Spotlight

He must be a significant person in the biblical record; 2 Kings, 2 Chronicles, and Isaiah all tell his story. Like many of the parallel accounts in the gospels, the stories are not identical, but together they provide a fascinating study of a significant and heroic individual. Most Christians know little about this person, Hezekiah, king of Judah. Try taking a poll in your Sunday school class or Bible study group sometime. You will probably find that eight out of ten remember nothing about Hezekiah. They might guess Hezekiah is the author of one of the Old Testament books. They're wrong.

It's a pity so few know about Hezekiah, since his story contains some thrilling and inspiring lessons. His life story fits well in this chapter on the challenges of serving in high office. In a number of ways, Hezekiah's story parallels that of Jehoshaphat, another little-known hero of the Old Testament. They both headed up the government in the kingdom of Judah, with its capital in Jerusalem. They were fathered by ungodly men and both spent the first years of their reign turning the Hebrews back to the worship of Jehovah God and getting rid of pagan practices of the people. They each had shortcomings, but unlike most other kings of Judah and Israel, they were successful politically and spiritually. Each of them experienced a dramatic and miraculous deliverance from their enemies by trusting fully in God instead of in the military strength of their nation.

It would be tempting to tell only the good parts of Hezekiah's story. We would do that if we were his public relations agents. But we can also learn from his mistakes in the same way we learn from his ancestor, King David.

Consider the good parts of Hezekiah's story:

Hezekiah was absolutely committed to God and did everything he could to lead the people of his kingdom back to godly living. This part of Hezekiah's life does not translate directly into the life of the government leader in most countries today. The kingdoms of Israel and Judah were meant to be theocracies. Separation of church and state did not exist. National life centered on worship and the king was to be first and foremost a spiritual leader. After the division of the Hebrew nation all the kings of Israel and most of the kings of the other half of the original kingdom, Judah, led in the wrong direction spiritually. Instead of leading toward obedience and worship of God as prescribed in Jehovah's covenant, these ungodly kings looked for all the deities they could find among the surrounding pagan people. They found plenty.

The few good kings worked overtime to replace the worship of the pagan gods with the worship of Jehovah in the temple. The account of this process of spiritual restoration and renewal under Hezekiah's leadership occupies two entire chapters in 2 Chronicles. The people had desecrated the temple and neglected the routines of worship; the Jewish priests no longer remembered how to lead worship. Getting back to square one became a huge task. Hezekiah's father, Ahaz, had stripped the temple of the items used in worship, locked up the building, and replaced the sacred symbols with their pagan counterparts. Cleansing the national spirit of all this ugly paganism proved to be a huge job. In Jewish practice people prepared burnt offerings to express repentance and seek cleansing. Under Hezekiah's leadership, they sacrificed six hundred bulls and three thousand sheep and goats, so many that the priests had to deputize some people to help in preparing the offerings (2 Chronicles 29:1-36).

The next step in renewing the spiritual life of the land surpassed the impressive temple cleansing and sacrifices. Observance of the annual Passover festival had been neglected as a result of the spiritual poverty of the Hebrews and their leaders. Hezekiah sent out an invitation to a massive Passover celebration that attracted not only the people of Judah, but worshipers from Israel and neighboring lands as well. The turnout was overwhelming and the spirit of the people jubilant. They expressed their joy in singing, celebrating, and solemn praying. Between the times of worship during the seven days of Passover, the people directed their zeal toward destroying the remaining pagan idols around Jerusalem. So great was the spiritual fervor that the people responded generously when King Hezekiah called on them to bring their offerings from the blessings God had given them — livestock, food, gold, and silver (2 Chronicles 30:1-25).

When the Passover festival neared its end some felt it should be extended, so the celebration was continued another seven days. The numbers of livestock sacrificed continued to grow, reaching literally into the tens of thousands. The summary comment in 2 Chronicles captures the exuberance of the people and God's joyful response:

> There was great joy in Jerusalem, for since the days of Solomon son of David king of Israel there had been nothing like this in Jerusalem. The priests and the Levites stood to bless the people, and God heard them, for their prayer reached heaven, his holy dwelling place. (2 Chronicles 30:26-27)

Clearly King Hezekiah was the prime mover in this incredible national revival. He initiated it and supported it with his resources. God greatly blessed him for his part in this significant turning back to God. In everything he undertook in the service of God's temple and in obedience to the law and the commands, he sought his God and worked wholeheartedly. And so he prospered (2 Chronicles 31:20-21).

It was like having Billy Graham as president of the United States—this was revival like the world had never seen. The godly king Hezekiah deserves much of the credit.

When faced with an overwhelming military threat, Hezekiah called on the only possible source of deliverance, the direct intervention of an all-powerful God. Kings and presidents win their greatest popularity in times when their nation is threatened from the outside. If they successfully face and defeat the enemy, they become national heroes and other failings are overlooked. The greater the threat, the greater the gain in their national support. If they falter in a time of military crisis, they lose the confidence of the people and no amount of domestic success will offset their weak image.

If great crises produce great leaders, Hezekiah had a perfect opportunity. A few years into his reign, the Assyrians attacked, defeated, and deported the Hebrews from the kingdom of Israel. This was not a good omen. Then Sennacherib, King of Assyria, began attacking the cities of Judah itself. Even well-fortified cities were no match for the Assyrian siege tactics. The Assyrians had huge battering rams to break down gates. By the Assyrian accounts, they carried off two hundred thousand Judean occupants of these defeated cities. It might have seemed like a good time for Hezekiah to go spend some time in his vacation place on the Mediterranean, but he had no intention of surrendering to the Assyrians. He strengthened Jerusalem's defenses, put the weapon makers on overtime, and even did what he could to sabotage the water supplies for the besieging armies. But Hezekiah's message to the people signaled clearly that he placed his trust not in these defense preparations but in a much greater defender:

> "Be strong and courageous. Do not be afraid or discouraged
> because of the king of Assyria and the vast army with him, for
> there is a greater power with us than with him. With him is
> only the arm of flesh, but with us is the Lord our God to help
> us and to fight our battles." (2 Chronicles 32:7-8)

When the establishment of a siege around Jerusalem did not frighten King Hezekiah, the Assyrians executed a clever propa-

Senator Mark Hatfield on his call to politics and to Christ

"This boyhood dream developed later into an earnest desire to become a politician, and all my education was directed to that end. I became more practical as the years passed and began adopting certain rules for political success.

"I made the choice that night, many years ago; I *committed* myself to Christ. I saw that for thirty-one years I had lived for self, and I decided I wanted to live the rest of my life for Jesus Christ. I asked God to forgive my self-centeredness and to make me his own. I was assured by the words of Paul, 'Therefore if any man be in Christ, he is a new creature: old things are passed away; behold, all things are become new' (2 Corinthians 5:17).

"Now, the decisions, the policies, and the program which I follow in my official life I try to root first of all in prayer. I believe that the Lord is interested in leading in this important job, and I depend upon him for counsel. This does not mean that every decision I make is the right one, that every policy which I have is the correct one; but I feel that these matters are of such importance that I do commit them to the Lord. When they are wrong, they are errors in my judgment and not his, and they are perhaps examples of where I tried to get ahead of God's leading."[39]

ganda campaign. It began with messages to Hezekiah, ridiculing his determination to trust in God. When that did not work, the Assyrians tried to undermine the people's confidence. The Assyrians made a point of telling the Judeans in their own language how foolish it would be to follow King Hezekiah when all he had to offer were empty assurances that God would deliver them. Day after day the propaganda war continued and day after day the people listened to Hezekiah's advice that they ignore the words and remain firm in their trust of God.

No amount of public courage and clever rebuttals of the Assyrians' harassment would have delivered Judah, and Hezekiah knew that well. He turned to God. He sought assurance through the prophet Isaiah, asking how to respond to Sennacherib's blasphemous defiance of Jehovah. God gave the words for that response:

> "But I know where you stay and when you come and go and
> how you rage against me. Because you rage against me and
> your insolence has reached my ears, I will put my hook in your
> nose and my bit in your mouth, and I will make you return by
> the way you came." (2 Kings 19:27-28)

If Sennacherib had had good sense he would have abandoned the siege and headed home when Isaiah delivered those words from God. Fortunately for the Hebrews, Sennacherib did not have good sense. It seemed to him that Hezekiah had nothing to sustain him but words of trust in God and a lot of praying. But what a person of prayer Hezekiah was! Such a great prayer offered by one of the great rulers of history deserves to be heard in its entirety:

> "O Lord, God of Israel, enthroned between the cherubim, you
> alone are God over all the kingdoms of the earth. You have
> made heaven and earth. Give ear, O Lord, and hear; open your
> eyes, O Lord, and see; listen to the words Sennacherib has sent
> to insult the living God. It is true, O Lord, that the Assyrian
> kings have laid waste these nations and their lands. They have
> thrown their gods into the fire and destroyed them, for they
> were not gods but only wood and stone, fashioned by men's
> hands. Now, O Lord our God, deliver us from his hand, so that
> all kingdoms on earth may know that you alone, O Lord, are
> God." (2 Kings 19:15-19)

The outcome of the confrontation between Hezekiah and Sennacherib was elegantly simple. Without using the kinds of special tactics of Joshua's strange army, Gideon's unconventional defense, and Jehoshaphat's singing soldiers, God miraculously intervened. God's angel did not even need the help of Hezekiah's armies to win the battle. The body count the next day was Assyrians, 185,000; Hebrews, 0. Not all the Assyrians were killed. Enough lived to pack their things and head home to Nineveh to

William Wilberforce on using our talents to serve God

"For true Christians, bodily and mental faculties, their naturally acquired abilities, their substance, their authority, their time, and their influence, are not instruments of their own gratification; these belong and are consecrated to the honor of God, and are employed in His service. This is the master principle to which every other must be subordinate. Whatever may previously have been the ruling passion, whatever their leading pursuit was before, whether sensual, or intellectual, whether of science, or taste, of fancy, or of feeling–it is now of minor importance in comparison. In point of fact the passion exists only at the pleasure of its true and legitimate Master, and its owner places it entirely under His direction and control."[40]

tell their countrymen it would not be a good idea to mount another attack on Jerusalem. And while Sennacherib was praying to the Assyrian gods his sons killed him (Isaiah 37:36-38).

Hezekiah called on God when a potentially fatal illness threatened his life. Godly leaders can call on God for personal as well as national needs. After the nation's amazing deliverance from the Assyrians, Hezekiah's struggle with physical problems seems anticlimactic. But in as much personal danger as the entire nation had been he felt he didn't have long to live. The king who trusted God in a national emergency also trusted God when he faced death. The God of mercy used Isaiah to deliver a message that Hezekiah's life would be extended by 15 years. Other accounts of healing in the Bible do not specify a specific span of time that God would provide continued good health. Another unusual element of this healing was a miraculous movement of the sun's shadow, assuring Hezekiah that the all-powerful God had healed him and would bless his life during his remaining years.

It would be nice if Hezekiah had served God consistently all his life. He had some great victories but like King David, he did stupid things. The Bible gives us the ugly with the beautiful in the accounts of people who accomplished great things.

Hezekiah's problems were principally of two kinds:
Before Hezekiah fully placed his trust in God for deliverance he tried a senseless alternative, paying tribute to the Assyrians. This reminds us that our wealth is not the source of our strength. We should not be too hard on Hezekiah; the northern Hebrew kingdom had already been wiped out. The Assyrians had defeated all the major cities in Judah except Jerusalem. If there was any hope that the enemy might withdraw, exchanging some gold and silver for the lives of his remaining countrymen seemed to make good sense to Hezekiah. But there were some problems. First, Hezekiah had to remove all the gold and silver from the temple in order to come up with enough precious metal to satisfy the Assyrians. This was a horrible denial of all the Jews had done to restore the worship of Jehovah to its rightful place in the nation. Second, resorting to tribute and bribery was a very poor substitute for complete trust in God. Third, no thinking person would have hoped Sennacherib would withdraw from conquering the stronghold of the Hebrews, the holy city of Jerusalem. Hezekiah should have saved the gold and silver (2 Kings 18:13-16).

Hezekiah's second failing also had to do with money, showing off the national treasuries to enemy officials. There was no good reason for Hezekiah to do what he did. God had just healed him and extended his life. He still lived in the glow of God's wonderful defeat of the Assyrians. He did not need to impress the visiting delegation of Babylonians. But amazingly, Hezekiah gave the group a complete tour of all the stockpiled national wealth. He led them through the Fort Knox of the day. *What were you thinking, Hezekiah?*

But read between the lines a little. The Assyrians had conquered the Babylonians and the Babylonians were looking for a chance to fight back. They were shopping around among the enemies of Assyria for potential allies in a coalition to overthrow the Assyrian Empire. They were not just taking a tour of the holdings of the rich and famous of the Middle East. The Babylonians might well have asked Hezekiah if he had enough resources to help mount a serious campaign against the Assyrians. Hezekiah, the expert in trusting God, had a major lapse that day. He should have told the Babylonians that no amount of wealth would make any difference against such a huge empire; it would only be successful if God was behind the effort against the Assyrians. But Hezekiah didn't do that.

The Babylonian delegation had barely left Jerusalem before the prophet Isaiah headed to the palace. Hezekiah could see he was not happy, but Hezekiah didn't catch on at first. Could it be that Isaiah was just curious about the mission of the visitors? Hezekiah calmly answered Isaiah's questions about the identity of the visitors, their mission, and what Hezekiah had told them and shown them. Hezekiah was painfully honest by saying he had shown the visitors everything of value in Jerusalem. Hezekiah didn't see anything wrong with that. After all, these important visitors from Babylon liked the Assyrians even less than the Jews.

But Hezekiah soon caught on as Isaiah delivered the heart of his message. Not only had it been completely inappropriate to show the guests the national treasures, but it was clear that this had been done out of pride and misplaced trust. It was like the time David angered God by ordering that the nation's troops be counted. Isaiah let Hezekiah off easy. He might have suggested God was going to take back those 15 bonus years but Isaiah's bad news was aimed at the people as a whole, not just at Hezekiah.

Isaiah said it made no sense whatever to value material things, for these things could never give them protection. They had seen that God could easily deliver the Jews from terrible danger, but it would not be done by their material strength. In fact, Isaiah's message echoed the messages from a big succession of godly prophets. Unless the Hebrews turned back to God they would be conquered and carried off into captivity. God had delivered them miraculously, but only because they had placed their complete trust in him. Isaiah had to deliver the sad news that the godly trust previously expressed by Hezekiah and the people would fade away and the dark side of the covenant would become a reality. Jerusalem would be destroyed (2 Kings 20:12-18).

When I was growing up I heard many sermons calling on the listeners to surrender themselves fully to God and to offer their lives and talents for God's service. Almost always that service was placed in a hierarchy of worth. Way at the top was the call to foreign missionary service. Next was "home missions," evangelism, and church planting. Then came pastoral ministry. That may well reflect the high value God places on those who serve him in these ways. But I cannot remember any sermons that raised the possibility that godly people might be called to serve God in the "full-time service" of government and politics. Not until I got to college did I begin to hear about the possibility of serving God in those endeavors. And not until I first heard Senator Hatfield speak at our college did it occur to me that his was a high and holy calling.

This is strange, considering the kinds of people whose lives we have examined in these chapters—biblical heroes such as Joseph, Gideon, Jehoshaphat, David, Nehemiah, and Hezekiah. In one way or another, these were people called of God and blessed by God to devote their talents and energies to serving God in the government. Why have they not been lifted up as role models for men and women who sense a call to public service? Why might a person with a call to politics have to be apologetic about this call around those who only see a value in "full-time Christian service"? It is easier to ask those questions than to answer them. But we would do well to reflect on the example of King Hezekiah, God's "full-time servant" in government. He had a couple of significant failings, but he accomplished wonderful things while he remained focused on God's power and God's deliverance. He set a great example for those who have responded to God's call to full-time political/Christian service. As God used William Wilberforce and Mark Hatfield, so he used Hezekiah in amazing ways.

MEET DAVID RAWSON

Some individuals are given the title of "ambassador" as a reward for past political contributions and loyalty. They may be fine people, but they have not "paid their dues" in a diplomatic service career. They have been perceptive or fortunate enough to win the favor of a person who as president of the United States can appoint them to a diplomatic post whether they have experience in that area or not. Other ambassadors earn their positions through their many years in diplomatic service and their expertise in a particular region of the world. David Rawson is an example of the latter. Before retiring from the U.S. foreign service, he served as ambassador in two African countries, Mali and Rwanda. Prior to that, he had earned a doctorate in political science and had worked his way up through the ranks in the State Department.

Rawson became interested in diplomatic service as a boy growing up in Burundi, in central Africa. He learned the local language, Kirundi, and learned about some of the issues that divided the two major ethnic groups in Burundi, the Hutu and the Tutsi. He also learned what it meant to be a faithful follower of Jesus, in part through the example of his father, Perry Rawson, a Friends missionary doctor. And he learned that it was important to bring the colonial era to an end, but that independence could not remove the economic and ethnic struggles countries such as Burundi had experienced.

Speaking at commencement events at George Fox University in May 2003, David Rawson told of some events in his diplomatic career that illustrated the need for the Christian virtue of mercy. One of these occurred while he was on an assignment with the State Department in Washington, D.C. He had become a part of the Bible study and prayer groups sponsored by the National Prayer Breakfast movement. Whether he was in Washington or in some other national capital, he had made a point of participating in the small groups. Some participants were firmly committed to Christ as Savior and Lord and others wouldn't call themselves believers but wanted to learn more about the values of prayer and Bible study.

In this particular prayer group the guest of honor was Pierre Buyoya, president of Burundi. Rawson's knowledge of Kirundi was pressed into service to interpret for President Buyoya. A prayer circle with joined hands concluded the Bible study and fellowship time. Rawson was at Buyoya's side and as he reached out to join hands with the president he suddenly was hit by the awful memories of close friends of his in Burundi who were rounded up and killed for no other reason than that they were Hutu. This man at his side, whose hand he was now holding, was a Tutsi. Though he was not personally responsible for the killing of Rawson's friends, he represented the group that had held power much of the time since independence. God touched Rawson that night as he and the head of state held hands. To pray together in Christian fellowship in that circle was to extend the forgiveness of Jesus for the violence of the past.

Rawson recounts another event from his career that had a much less happy outcome than the circle of prayer and acceptance. As U.S. Ambassador to Rwanda, he had worked for months in support of discussions that aimed toward a peaceful resolution of the intense hostilities of the Hutu and Tutsi, the same two ethnic groups he had come to know as a young man in Burundi. His knowledge of Kirundi from his boyhood was helpful, since Rwanda's language, Kinyarwanda, is very similar to Kirundi. Rawson had hoped that United Nations peacekeeping personnel could be brought in to support some kind of agreement between the Tutsi and Hutu. Then as he sat in his living room in Rwanda's capital, Kigali, he heard a terrible explosion. It turned out that the sound came from the destruction of an airplane carrying Rwanda's president, Jevenal Habyarimana, along with the president of Burundi, Cyprien Ntaryamira. The airplane and the entire peace process went up in flames that day, putting an end to Rawson's efforts to find a means of sharing power between the two ethnic groups.

Former ambassador Rawson tells about the awful feeling of having to shift his focus from helping the peace process to evacuating Americans from the country. With the Americans safely out of the country, Rawson returned to the United States. He went to church the next Sunday and found the words of the liturgy sadly relevant that day: "We confess that we have too much followed the designs and intents of our own hearts." All he could do was plead for God's mercy because his efforts toward peace had not been successful and the people about whom he cared so much were on a rampage of ethnic slaughter.

David Rawson's calling has been one of global public service. Now as a college professor he can help his students see past the oversimplifications found in textbooks. He challenges them to find their place in public service around the world.

CHAPTER SIXTEEN

Answering the Call to Active Citizenship

Solomon's inauguration had not been much of an event. What it lacked in planning and preparations, the people provided in enthusiasm and zeal (see chapter 1). David's son impressed them with his potential to be a great national leader. When it was time for a much more significant day of celebration, the dedication of the temple in Jerusalem, the people were still impressed with and supportive of Solomon.

When David, Solomon's father, first discussed his plan to build a temple with the prophet Nathan, they agreed it was the right thing to do. David's heart was in the right place. He was uncomfortable living in a beautiful palace while only a tent sheltered the Ark of the Covenant, one of the sacred representations of God's presence. Who could object to the idea of building an appropriate place for God's people to worship? But the next day David saw the same look on Nathan's face he had seen during the painful encounter about Bathsheba. Sure enough, Nathan had a word from the Lord—David was not to build the temple. Solomon's father had felt great disappointment when God told him he was not to build the temple (1 Chronicles 17:3-14).

Hadn't God fully forgiven David for his adultery and murder? Hadn't David paid the price through the terrible death of the first child born to him and Bathsheba? Yes, it is clear from the Scripture that God fully forgave David for his wrong and foolish behavior. God's decision to withhold the privilege of building the temple had to do with where David placed his trust. Apparently David had begun to see his reign as an extension of the killing of the giant Goliath. Instead of trusting God to take care of the nation's enemies, as Gideon, Hezekiah, and Jehoshaphat later did, David began to think the power to kill giants and defeat national enemies was found in his own skill as a military strategist and the power of the nation's armies.

God told David he was not to build the temple because he had made militarism the central feature of his reign (1 Chronicles 22:8-9). David heard that message but did not fully understand, for soon he ordered his commander in chief to count up the nation's armies. Numbering the troops seemed harmless enough, but even General Joab realized it was an affront to God. It was like saying the nation's only significant source of strength was military. "Let's find out how many soldiers we have, so we can be sure we can defeat all our enemies." David's sin of not fully trusting God was as serious as his adultery and murder, and the punishment was worse. Seventy thousand people died in a plague God sent to get the point across to David (1 Chronicles 21:1-15).

Now as our story continues, David was dead. Solomon had made a wonderful start as king. He humbly sought God's wisdom and discernment and God honored his request and blessed him. His father had tried to achieve greatness as a warrior, but Solomon found his greatness as a builder and a leader for peace. He knew how important the building of a temple had been to his father, so he made that the first priority in his reign. He spared no expense. The design preserved the layout of the tabernacle the Hebrews had carried with them during the Exodus and after their arrival in Palestine. But everywhere one looked gold and ornate accessories adorned the new temple. Solomon used the word *magnificent* to describe it and he did not exaggerate (1 Chronicles 4—6).

Senator Mark Hatfield on the need for spiritual renaissance

"And since, thank God, you cannot legislate the hearts or minds of any people, I believe a spiritual renaissance is critical to those who make up our nation. By spiritual renaissance I mean revolution, a grassroots revolution sparking within each heart, leading us in new directions that, for instance, can lead to harmonious relationships with all those around us—rather than into repetitive bloodshed. What a culture we could create if we focused on intrinsic, loving, human values rather than consumption, selfishness, and disregard for life.

"Define your own spiritual commitment. Encourage your conscience. Use loving spirituality to infuse your personal, public, and political acts. Take advantage of spiritual stewardship when dealing with political issues such as the environment, the needs of humans, the dangers of war. Demonstrate commitment by actions which address the needs of humans, not actions which destroy. Find like-minded friends, encourage one another and build support as you would a living cell. Your spirit will multiply as naturally as the cells within us all."[41]

The day had come for the dedication of the temple. Without question, it marked the high point of the reign of one of the most impressive government leaders in human history. The dedication began with a solemn procession of priests carrying the Ark of the Covenant to the special place prepared for it in the temple. The high priest entered that place, called the Holy of Holies as in the tabernacle, only once a year to offer atoning sacrifices for the sins of the people. While the priests brought the ark to its place, singers and instrumentalists joined in praise to God for this great event. The text of the music was elegantly simple: "He is good; his love endures forever." God placed his blessing on the completed temple by filling it with a cloud, reminiscent of the cloud that symbolized God's presence and direction during the Exodus (2 Chronicles 5:2-14).

The ark stood in its place and the people crowded around to see one of the greatest events of their history. It was time for King Solomon to begin the actual dedication process. He made his way to the top of the platform he had built in the middle of the outer courtyard and waited for the crowd to become quiet. An amazing dedication program followed, including Solomon's opening remarks, a very long and powerful dedication prayer, the offering of massive numbers of livestock, more music, tearful prayers of thanksgiving to God, and boisterous celebrating. After all the festivities were completed and the people had gone home, God responded to the prayers and the completion of the temple with a personal message of affirmation to Solomon.

A number of statements embedded in the text of the temple dedication speech, the prayer, and God's response to the temple's completion provide an appropriate finale to our study of active Christian citizenship. The words in the speeches and prayers were not just religious in content; this was as much a political event as a religious one. The people of the nation came together to reaffirm that they found their strength only in God. David had tried the tactics of the world's ways, placing his trust in armies. Solomon came forward to say that placing the temple at the center of the kingdom symbolized a renewed trust in God, a fresh start toward being a people God could protect and bless.

Looking at the rhetoric of the temple dedication day, we find these points that summarize the call to active Christian citizenship:

✓ **Individually, we must respond to the opportunities God gives us and accept the things we are not permitted to do.** Solomon reminded the audience that it was David's desire to build the temple, but God did not permit him to do that. Solomon did not condemn his father for the faults that had stood in the way of building the temple (2 Chronicles 6:4-11). But the people there that day would have known the reason. David had put his ultimate faith in the nation's armies, not in God's power. A door was closed for David and opened for Solomon. In our lives as Christian

William Wilberforce on greatness

"In fact, instead of it being true that the prevalence of real religion would produce a stagnation of life, it is in reality true that it would infallibly produce the reverse. A man would be given a new motive to carry on his vocation with vigor, whatever his employment or pursuit. It would be a motive more sustaining and dynamic than any he had by merely humanistic perspectives. His foremost concern would not be so much to succeed as it would be to have a principled life before God. So he would not be liable to the same disappointments as men who are active in labor for worldly gain or fame. And thus he would possess the true secret of a life that was both useful and happy.

"However the external effects may vary, the internal principle is the same. It is the despotism in each one to make self the great center and end of his desires and pleasures. It is the tendency to overrate his own merits and importance, and of course to magnify his claims on others and to underrate theirs on him. It is the disposition to undervalue the advantages and to overstate the disadvantages of his condition in life. The opposite to selfishness is public spirit. This is the great principle of public life—which keeps it active and vigorous and which carries it to true greatness and glory."[42]

citizens, some will have great opportunities, perhaps on the scale of those opened to Wilberforce and Hatfield, and others will be given less impressive places of service.

✓ **Individually and nationally, we are in a covenant relationship with God, able to receive God's blessing only as we are obedient to God.** The covenant theme is woven throughout the dedication speech and prayer. The priests had just placed the sacred Ark of the Covenant in the new temple. The very nature of the temple served as a symbol of God's promises to his people and the associated requirement that people obey God. In his prayer, Solomon called on God to keep the kingdom intact (2 Chronicles 6:14-17). Solomon was really praying that his descendants keep their part of the covenant. There was no question that God would do his part to bless the nation if the people would be obedient and faithful. Contemporary political history is littered with people who violated their sacred trust as leaders and chose to act illegally and immorally for their own self-gratification. The call to active citizenship asks us to carry out God's covenant of faithfulness in that with which we are entrusted.

✓ **A central function of active citizenship is to serve as reconcilers, individually and internationally.** Solomon's prayer addressed the need for leaders and citizens to deal appropriately with disputes between people, one of the central functions of governments. That process involves not only the determination of guilt and innocence, but restoring right relationships between the victim and the offender. Internationally, Solomon prayed that the people would learn from the conflicts with other nations and would discern ways to approach those disputes in a spirit of repentance, not arrogance. Solomon even prayed that the Hebrews would be able to see potential for repentance and godly behavior in their national enemies. This implies that those once thought to be enemies can become allies and friends (2 Chronicles 6:22-25, 34-35).

✓ **Governments operate as guardians of scarce resources. The effective citizen compassionately addresses the needs of the people of the land.** Solomon acknowledged in his prayer that the Hebrews could expect droughts, crop failures caused by diseases and insects, and other disasters. Solomon prayed for God's help when the people experienced these events, but he also realized that he, as king, and all the people should be ready to respond to the needs arising out of these unfortunate events. Solomon might have had in mind the way God had spared the lives of the Hebrews and Egyptians during a terrible drought and would have understood his own role as a leader in addressing similar needs (2 Chronicles 6:26-28).

✓ **Governments exist to meet the needs of individuals — both citizens of the nation and those who are part of the nation but not citizens.** Solomon asked God to help those people who would have special needs and in so praying was committing himself to extend help to such people. Senator Hatfield has said many times that one of his most important functions as a public official was to use his influence on behalf of individual constituents who needed help to gain the assistance of the government. Solomon expressed remarkable compassion for those who were not Hebrews but who were living among them and who had a variety of needs. Many Jews felt they had no obligation to help their neighbors who were not Jews. Solomon prayed on behalf of the minority groups and the aliens (2 Chronicles 6:29-33). His prayer reminds us of the lifelong struggle of William Wilberforce for those of his day who were "foreigners," who were given no more respect than animals, i.e., African slaves.

After Solomon completed his marvelous prayer, after the people were dismissed to their homes, the temple area had been cleaned up, and the musical instruments put away, God came to Solomon during the night with a wonderful message of assurance and warning. Its beginning statement may have seemed a little anticlimactic at the time: "I have heard your prayer and have chosen this place for myself as a temple for sacrifices." There follows another expression of the covenant, one that well deserves to be quoted regularly as a reminder of our need for repentance and obedience to God:

> "If my people, who are called by my name, will humble
> themselves and pray and seek my face and turn from their
> wicked ways, then will I hear from heaven and will forgive
> their sin and will heal their land."

Those are heartwarming words, but God went on to assure Solomon that the covenant always has two dimensions. God would bless them as they obeyed him and most definitely would withhold his blessing if they turned away from him (2 Chronicles 7:11-22).

The sequel to God's response to the temple dedication involved an interesting person, the Queen of Sheba, thought to be from a kingdom in the southern part of the Arabian peninsula. The queen visited Solomon to determine for herself if he was as great as his reputation indicated. She was overwhelmed with all she saw and experienced in Jerusalem. Significantly, it was not the size of his armies, nor the splendor of his palace and the temple that captured her attention. She was interested primarily in Solomon's intellectual and spiritual strength and could not get over the depth of his giftedness. She offered a fitting tribute during her visit that would do well as a framed motto for the active Christian citizen:

> "Praise be to the Lord your God, who has delighted in you and placed you on his throne as king to rule for the Lord your God. Because of the love of your God for Israel and his desire to uphold them forever, he has made you king over them, to maintain justice and righteousness." (2 Chronicles 9:8)

It would be nice if we could avoid mentioning that Solomon eventually turned away from the high ideals he expressed at the time of the temple dedication. In fact, one of the compilers of the historical books chose to do that. The account in 2 Chronicles has a happy ending, with nothing but good news about Solomon's effectiveness as king and the indescribable prosperity of the kingdom. But the Bible does not hide the failings of even the greatest of the leaders. First Kings records the sad story of his later years and the horrible way he turned away from God. It would be convenient to blame it on his wives and mistresses, as the account seems to do, but of course he was the one who made wrong choices, one after the other. It was he who decided to explore the religions of the women he married and to begin to practice these other faiths. It was he who seemed to conclude it was too limiting to serve only one God. Surely he could learn things from other value systems. But it was idolatry, not tolerance, for which God judged Solomon (1 Kings 11:1-25).

Solomon had to receive the depressing news that the kingdom would be shattered by internal rebellion and the peace that had characterized his reign would come to a violent end. How sad to read about Solomon's last days, but there is no way to avoid the consequences of violating God's covenant. And there is no way to talk about being a godly citizen today without being honest about those who have been victims of their own pride, lust, and arrogance. Solomon's legacy in the form of political and moral failure continues.

Solomon ended his life in failure, but his words of wisdom still bless and challenge us. A selection from Proverbs provides a fitting conclusion to our study of active Christian citizenship:

> Does not wisdom call out? Does not understanding raise her voice?
>
> On the heights along the way, where the paths meet, she takes her stand;
>
> beside the gates leading into the city, at the entrances she cries aloud:
>
> "To you, O men, I call out; I raise my voice to all mankind.
>
> All the words of my mouth are just; none of them is crooked or perverse.
>
> To the discerning all of them are right; they are faultless to those who have knowledge.
>
> To fear the Lord is to hate evil; I hate pride and arrogance, evil behavior and perverse speech.
>
> Counsel and sound judgment are mine; I have understanding and power.
>
> By me kings reign and rulers make laws that are just;
>
> by me princes govern, and all nobles who rule on earth.
>
> Blessed is the man who listens to me, watching daily at my doors, waiting at my doorway.
>
> For whoever finds me finds life and receives favor from the Lord." (Proverbs 8:1-4, 8-9, 13-16, 34-35)

NOTES

1. Bruce Wilkinson, *The Prayer of Jabez* (Sisters, Oregon: Multnomah Press, 2000).

2. Parker J. Palmer, *The Courage to Teach: Exploring the Inner Landscape of a Teacher's Life* (San Francisco: Jossey-Bass Publishers), 102-103.

3. Lon Fendall, *William Wilberforce: Abolitionist, Politician, Writer* (Barbour Books, 2002).

4. William Wilberforce, *Real Christianity Contrasted with the Prevailing Religious System* (Portland, Oregon: Multnomah Press, 1982).

5. Hatfield, "The Christian and the State," edited transcript of the discussion, published in *Christianity Today*, June 21, 1963, 10.

6. Wilberforce, *Real Christianity*, 130-131.

7. Mark O. Hatfield, *Between a Rock and a Hard Place* (Waco, Texas: Word Books, 1976), 72.

8. Wilberforce, *Real Christianity*, 130-131.

9. Dr. Karin Jordan is director of the graduate program in counseling at George Fox University. She presented this testimony at the Newberg Area Mayors' Prayer Breakfast on May 18, 2002.

10. Hatfield, *Between a Rock and a Hard Place*, 72.

11. Arthur O. Roberts, *Let the Spirit Soar: The Mayoral Poems of Arthur O. Roberts* (Yachats, Oregon: City of Yachats, 2000), 29. [See my chapter 7 for information about Arthur Roberts.]

12. Hatfield, *Between a Rock and a Hard Place*, 72.

13. There are those who have extended their conscientious objection to militarism to the refusal to pay the portion of their taxes that would go for military programs. This clearly is an exception to the principle stated here. There is not a specific basis for this non-payment of taxes in the Bible, but it is consistent with godly civil disobedience, discussed in another part of the book.

14. Roberts, *Let the Spirit Soar*, 31.

15. Wilberforce, *Real Christianity*, 9.

16. Mark O. Hatfield, *Conflict and Conscience* (Waco, Texas: Word Books), 149, 156-157.

17. Hatfield, introduction to Wilberforce's *Real Christianity*, xxiv.

18. Wilberforce, *Real Christianity*, 92, 109.

19. Hatfield, *Conflict and Conscience*, 41.

20. Wilberforce, *Real Christianity*, 106.

21. Roberts, *Let the Spirit Soar*, 3.

22. Hatfield, *Conflict and Conscience*, 33, 39-40, 170.

23. Wilberforce, *Real Christianity*, 105-106.

24. Hatfield, *Conflict and Conscience*, 47.

25. Wilberforce, *Real Christianity*, 50-51.

26. Wilberforce, *Real Christianity*, 54-55.

27. Hatfield, *Conflict and Conscience*, 157-159.

28. Adapted from an address at George Fox University commencement, May 1, 2002.

29. Hatfield, *Conflict and Conscience*, 114, 162.

30. Robert K. Greenleaf, *Servant Leadership,* Paulist Press, 1977.

31. Wilberforce, *Real Christianity*, 63-64.

32. Greenleaf, *Servant Leadership*, 13, 14.

33. Hatfield, *Between a Rock and a Hard Place*, 65-66.

34. Wilberforce, *Real Christianity*, 124.

35. Hatfield, *Conflict and Conscience,* 158.

36. Wilberforce, *Real Christianity*, 68.

37. Hatfield, *Conflict and Conscience,* 161.

38. Wilberforce, *Real Christianity*, 110.

39. Hatfield, *Conflict and Conscience*, 96-99.

40. Wilberforce, *Real Christianity*, 47.

41. Mark O. Hatfield, *Against the Grain: Reflections of a Rebel Republican* (Ashland, Oregon: White Cloud Press, 2001), 243, 245-246.

42. Wilberforce, *Real Christianity*, 106-107.

www.ingramcontent.com/pod-product-compliance
Lightning Source LLC
Chambersburg PA
CBHW030442290526
45786CB00001B/413